Y0-AEB-055

Caribbean Geopolitics

LACC Studies on Latin America and the Caribbean

Published with the Latin American and Caribbean Center,
Florida International University

Caribbean Geopolitics

Toward Security Through Peace?

Andres Serbin

translated by
Sabeth Ramirez

Lynne Rienner Publishers • Boulder & London

To my son Andrei,
with a shade of hope

Published in the United States of America in 1990 by
Lynne Rienner Publishers, Inc.
1800 30th Street, Boulder, Colorado 80301

and in the United Kingdom by
Lynne Rienner Publishers, Inc.
3 Henrietta Street, Covent Garden, London WC2E 8LU

Library of Congress Cataloging-in-Publication Data
Serbin, A. (Andres)
[Caribe, zona de paz? English]
Caribbean geopolitics : Toward security through peace? / Andres Serbin : translated by Sabeth Ramírez
p. cm.
Translation of: El Caribe, zona de paz?
Includes bibliographical references.
ISBN 1-55587-213-1
1. Caribbean Area—Politics and government—1945– 2. Geopolitics—Caribbean area. 3. Caribbean Area—Economic conditions—1945– 4. Caribbean Area—Military relations—Foreign countries.
I. Title
F2183.S4713 1990
320.9729—dc20 90-33398
CIP

British Cataloguing in Publication Data
A Cataloguing in Publication record for this book
is available from the British Library.

Printed and bound in the United States of America

The paper used in this publication meets the requirements
of the American National Standard for Permanence of
Paper for Printed Library Materials Z39.48-1984

Contents

Foreword

Juan Somavia

When the history of twentieth century Latin America is written, the third quarter will play a leading role. If history were to be written today, surely the key topics would be the unleashing of the Central American crisis; the Malvinas war; the external debt crisis; the spread of dictatorial regimes inspired by the National Security Doctrine and their subsequent replacement by unstable civilian governments; and finally, renewed efforts toward regional political cooperation, first through the Contadora Group and, more recently, through the Group of Eight. Moreover, an analysis of historical events would also include as a central phenomenon drugs and drug trafficking, a problem that concerns all states in the continent.

It is quite possible, however, that this hypothetical retrospective study would include very little data on the Caribbean countries—the island territories belonging geographically to what we generally call Latin America, and which are both part of yet distinct from the continent.

Any version of history would undoubtedly include the decolonization process in the Caribbean, with the emergence of the microstates as its most dominant feature. The process would probably be recognized as highly significant but in all likelihood there would be little substance to the discussion. The reader would learn very little.

Few people are knowledgeable about the Caribbean. Try answering the following questions, for example: How many countries are in the Caribbean? What are their names? Where are they?

Failure to answer these questions is characteristic not only of North Americans but of South and Central Americans as well. It demonstrates not only gaps in the educational curriculum for youth of nearly all countries but also another much more significant truth. Latin America is composed of several subregions, which exist in relative isolation and ignorance of each other.

The prevailing lack of knowledge about the Caribbean—and about what happens there—is worrisome, for the truth is that whatever happens or fails to happen in this area will directly affect peace and security in Latin America as a whole.

When the Secretariat of the South American Commission for Peace was established in Santiago de Chile in 1987, one of its priorities was to provide public leaders with objective information on peace and security conditions in Latin America and the Caribbean. This decision was taken as a logical result of the political will expressed in 1986 when the Organizing Committee for the commission was formed in Caracas, Venezuela. It was then proposed that the general goal of this new institution should be to promote the creation of a peace zone in Latin America and the Caribbean; and it was decided to focus in the first phase on South America.

The principal motivation of the various members of this commission is to promote regional political cooperation in order to facilitate and strengthen democratic processes in the region. Participants in the commission take as their starting point a commitment to democracy, and identify regional political cooperation for peace and security as the ideal framework for preventing public liberties from ever again falling prey to authoritarian temptations. In addition, participants seek common criteria for action so as to respond jointly to the difficulties and challenges they face in the international context.

The South American Commission for Peace is deeply convinced that Latin America requires a greater degree of autonomy in the international sphere in order successfully to cope with the serious problems confronting it. However, the commission also recognizes that Latin America neither acts nor behaves as a homogeneous entity. It is precisely this realization—this conviction that Latin America is a mosaic composed of multifarious realities—that has led us as commission members to propose approaching the problem step by step, recognizing subregional differences, and building on this basis a solid and lasting unity at the regional level.

These guidelines led to the proposal approved by the commission on June 8, 1988, in Montevideo, on the occasion of its Second Plenary Session. The proposal stated that a Latin American security system

> should be based on adequate identification of the shared and differentiated interests of South America, Central America and the Caribbean. It will develop progressively [it adds] as a result of the success achieved in each subregion in setting in motion Regional Democratic Security.

This book is a practical contribution toward knowledge of one of these subregions: the Caribbean. In the following pages, Andres Serbin introduces us to a world that most of us ignore. With great didactic ability, proceeding step by step, he outlines for us the shared and divergent characteristics and interests of the Caribbean countries as well as the interests of those countries that are extraregional actors in the area.

The book begins with a basic question: What exactly is understood by "Caribbean"? In the course of answering this question, the author must address the basic issues facing the region. In this way, he reviews the principal socioeconomic and political features of the Caribbean and provides us with an overall view.

The author's motivation is ultimately to determine the feasibility of implementing a peace zone in the Caribbean. A mature analysis, neither willful nor fatalistic, helps the reader evaluate not only the complexity of such an undertaking, but also the context within which it could be viable.

Andres Serbin demonstrates that the Caribbean is a subregion with its own particularities and characteristics. Its cultural diversity; its economic structures, highly dependent upon external factors; the presence of the former European colonial powers; the decisive role of the United States; the existence of socialist Cuba; and finally, the increasing participation in the region of Latin America's middle powers—Venezuela, Colombia, Mexico, and more recently, Brazil—are all elements that converge to define its unique personality. It is precisely against this background of particular socioeconomic, political, and geopolitical factors that successive proposals for a peace zone in the Caribbean have been formulated.

Eric Williams, prime minister of Trinidad and Tobago, in an address to his country's House of Representatives given in December 1963, was one of the first to promote the conversion of the Caribbean into a peace zone. The initiative, however, as Serbin points out, was taken up again in subsequent years only by scholars dedicated to the study of this part of America.

It was after the United Nations Special Session on Disarmament in 1978—which lent strong political support to the idea of establishing peace zones in various regions of the world as a contribution to planetary security—that a formal proposal was made to establish a peace zone in the Antilles. The proposal was put forth in October 1979, at the initiative of Grenada, when a formal resolution to establish a peace zone in the Caribbean was approved at the Twelfth Plenary Session of the General Assembly of the Organization of American States, held in La Paz, Bolivia.

The United States, however, ignored the OAS resolution, and in fact adopted a policy that unleashed an unprecedented militarization process and arms race in the region. U.S. policy was formulated in response, on the one hand, to Central American events, in particular the Sandinista revolution and the war in El Salvador, and on the other hand, to the Grenadan revolutionary process led by Maurice Bishop and the apparently leftist tendencies of the governments of Suriname and Guyana.

The resulting militarization process and arms race was relatively ignored by Latin American analysts, since the focus of concern during those years was the Central American crisis. Unfortunately, only the Grenada invasion was able to draw Latin American attention to the Caribbean processes. It is still not fully recognized in Latin America that, despite the particularities of each subregion, a close interrelationship exists among all the areas that make up the region.

Progress toward a peace zone in both Latin America and the Caribbean or, as a first stage, a peace zone in South America, is closely tied to the possibility of reactivating the 1979 proposal for a peace zone specifically in the Caribbean. Conditions of peace and security in the Caribbean area are conditioning factors for determining peace and security matters in the rest of the continent.

In the late 1980s, we were witness to a phenomenon that could well play a decisive role in making the region's dreams of a peace zone come true.

It is still impossible to foretell the significance for Latin America of events in the Soviet Union and in Eastern Europe. The profound sociopolitical and economic transformations occurring under Gorbachev's leadership have already resulted in some reduction in international tensions and the possibility of increased understanding between the Soviet Union and the United States. The structural effects of these changes within the Soviet Union upon the international system will have consequences for the insertion of Latin American and Caribbean countries into that system that are still impossible to predict. Present world trends may be conducive to higher degrees of international autonomy both in Latin America and the Caribbean as a whole and in each of their subregions. If the respective governments involved use their political will to channel this autonomy into stronger instruments for subregional and regional political cooperation, the obstacles faced until now in progressing toward a peace zone in the Caribbean may progressively be overcome.

Through this work, Andres Serbin has enabled us to identify the specific factors on which action should be based if the desire for peace and self-determination are to become reality in the Caribbean and indeed, in all of Latin America.

Juan Somavia
Secretary General
of the South American Peace Commission

Acknowledgments

This book was originally prepared in Spanish for the South American Commission for Peace, Regional Security, and Democracy, and was completed in May 1988. Some recent developments, such as the military coup that led to the overthrow of President Leslie Manigat in Haiti and its aftershocks, are not included. Although I feel that the essence of the analysis and the book's basic proposals and general conclusions remain valid today, I have added a chapter to update this English-language version, further analyzing the main trends in the region as it enters the 1990s.

This study was written during my year-long stay as Leverhulme Visiting Fellow at the Centre for Caribbean Studies, University of Warwick, and it was enriched by the comments and suggestions of friends and colleagues at several British universities. Among them I am especially indebted to Paul Sutton of the University of Hull for his cordial support and assistance, generous hospitality, and useful suggestions. I was also provided with an opportunity to discuss some of the key topics of the book with other researchers, and to benefit from their experience thanks to the kind invitation of Colin Clarke and Christian Girault of Oxford University and Roberto Espindola of the University of Bradford. Much of the documentation and bibliographical material was obtained at the libraries of the Institute of Strategic Studies and the Institute of Commonwealth Studies, in London.

I would like to thank Daniel van Euwen, current president of the European Association of Caribbean and Central American Studies (ASERCCA), for inviting me to give the keynote address at the association's annual meeting, on which the final chapter to the English version of this book is based. Finally, I want to acknowledge a very special debt to my colleagues at the Instituto Venezolano de Estudios Sociales y Políticos (INVESP), Francine Jacome, Carlos J. Moneta, and Carlos Romero, for their continuing (and patient) supply of information and materials from Caracas. To all of them, my deepest thanks for their assistance and backing.

A.S.

Introduction

Since the 1960s, many political events have converged to transform the Caribbean region into a zone with its own distinct geopolitical dynamics. Traditionally identified with Latin America as a whole, the Caribbean, during the subsequent three decades, created a political environment of its own in the Western Hemisphere, with a configuration clearly differentiated from that of either North or South America.

During the period following World War II, processes such as the evolution of Puerto Rico's political status, the Cuban revolution, U.S. intervention in the Dominican Republic in 1965, or even the persistence of the Duvalier dictatorship in Haiti were associated with situations originating in the Latin American community. As of 1962, however, new regional actors began to emerge and to participate actively both in the hemisphere and in the international system, mainly as a consequence of the process of decolonization of British and Dutch territories.

In addition, the Caribbean Basin acquired strategic and political prominence, which it had not previously enjoyed, as a result of the consolidation of the revolutionary process in Cuba, the overthrow of Somoza and the Sandinista victory in Nicaragua, and the civil war in El Salvador. The takeover by a socialist regime in Grenada and the emergence of governments in Jamaica, Guyana, and Suriname that also leaned toward socialism added to the region's new strategic importance. Extraregional actors that had traditionally been involved in the region now outlined specific policies toward the Caribbean Basin, and the area began progressively to distinguish itself from the rest of Latin America, by virtue of its potential for internal political conflict as well as its possible international impact.

At the same time, the middle powers in the region also began to gradually consolidate their "Caribbean" policies, starting with Cuba (which in the mid-1970s initiated a specific policy toward the non-Hispanic Caribbean) and continuing with the increasing involvement in the Caribbean of Mexico, Venezuela, Colombia, and more recently, Brazil. The Caribbean Basin has thus come to be regarded as a separate region in the hemisphere with its own geopolitical dynamics, which, though conditioned by the East-West confrontation, are nevertheless clearly affected by North-South issues.

However, the emergence of the region as a geopolitical area with its own diverse characteristics, subject to strategic and political considerations, has given rise to a particular set of issues. First, an internal distinction is made within the Basin between the Central American isthmus and the non-Hispanic and island Caribbean. The ethnohistorical and socioeconomic differences between these two clearly separate areas challenge the validity of a geopolitical definition that treats them as one.[1] In fact, a large variety of possible definitions of the region—based on distinct national, regional, political, and ethnohistorical interests—adds to the complexity of the issues.

On the other hand, the region's increasing strategic and geopolitical importance poses additional, less abstract questions related to the political vulnerability of the states that compose it. The Central American crisis and political events in the non-Hispanic Caribbean, most notably the 1983 Grenada invasion, have cast doubts on the region's economic viability as well, and demonstrated its vulnerability vis-à-vis processes and actors alien to its societies. Undertaking a careful study of these societies and their geopolitical insertion in the region, along with their regional and international relations, is therefore appropriate. Moreover, we will examine the concerns of regional leaders for development and socioeconomic progress, as well as their aspirations toward removing the Caribbean from the reach of superpower confrontation—concerns that geostrategic analyses of the Caribbean Basin have tended to overlook.

With these questions in mind, the first part of this book, following an introductory discussion of regional actors and definitions, attempts to outline the distinguishing features of development strategies implemented in the Caribbean and their social and political consequences, as well as the impact of international relations on these strategies, and attempts at regional integration and cooperation.

This is followed by a general description of the region's geopolitical scene, against a background of distinct sociopolitical features. In particular we will examine the arms race and militarization processes recently experienced by some Caribbean societies and the region as a whole. Then, we will analyze and assess, in the light of regional and extraregional factors, the viability of regional initiatives aimed at converting the Caribbean into a peace zone. Finally, in this English-language edition, we have added a chapter to present recent developments in the context of current global transformation.

The analysis stresses both endogenous and exogenous political and geostrategic factors, bearing in mind, however, as a basic assumption, that the root cause of the problems facing societies in the region is to be found in the vulnerability of their economies to external interests and in endemic socioeconomic conditions, such as poverty and unemployment. We approach our analysis primarily from a Latin American perspective, based on the fact that there is a general lack of knowledge about the non-Hispanic Caribbean in Latin American academic and political spheres, and since relations between Latin America and the Caribbean area will be increasingly important in years to come.[2]

In this regard, it should be pointed out that, owing to this relative ignorance about the non-Hispanic Caribbean, as compared, for example, to the much more widely known problems of such Caribbean societies as Cuba, Haiti, and the Dominican Republic (which are perceived as part of the Latin American community), the latters' foreign and domestic policies have been largely omitted in this book. This should not be understood as their being of lesser importance in the region.

Notes

1. Isabel Jaramillo: "Medio Oriente y 'Cuenca del Caribe': fuerza de paz o de intervención?", in *Cuadernos de Nuestra América,* vol. 1, no. 1, January-July 1984.

2. Andres Serbin: *Etnocentrismo y geopolitica. Percepciones y relaciones entre el Caribe de Habla inglesa y América Latina,* Academia Nacional de la Historia, Caracas, 1990.

1
Definitions, Development Strategies, and Initiatives for Integration and Cooperation

Definitions and Actors

Caribbean scholars and analysts frequently point out that it is predominantly history and not geography that divides the island countries of the Caribbean from each other and makes the area so complex.[1] Contemporary politics and international relations have rendered the situation even more complicated. However unwillingly, we have grown accustomed to seeing the region through narrow definitions and categories that have been validated over time but that very often do not agree with the region's geographic, historical, political, and economic reality. These categories and definitions have given rise to persistent myths concerning the region and its future.

Throughout its historical evolution, many names have been given to the area. The varying colonial contexts as well as the diverse cultural and political assumptions of the primary political actors involved have given rise to a wide variety of names for the region, from *Antilles* to *West Indies* to *Caribbean Basin.*

The differing historical assumptions about and perceptions of the area account for three distinct definitions that occur in discourse about the Caribbean.

First, the Caribbean Basin as a whole tends to be seen as a geostrategic area of influence affecting the United States. From this perspective, it is defined in geographic terms based on its weakest links: the Central American states and the island Caribbean, including Belize and the Guianas, all under the major influence of the United States.[2] This view of the area is held not only by the United States but also by its North Atlantic partners, including the former colonial powers, for whom the Caribbean is a particularly sensitive geostrategic and economic region. The Soviet bloc, in turn, has coined the term *Karibiiski Basein* to reflect a similar concept.

From the economic point of view, the increasing U.S. interest in the Caribbean Basin is tied to the fact that it is the fourth-largest market for U.S. products, accounting for 14 percent and 11 percent, respectively, of U.S. exports and imports.[3] Eighty-five percent of bauxite imports and 70 percent

Table 1.1 The Caribbean: Basic Data

Country or territory	*Area (km2)*	*Population*	*Adminstr. Links*	*Language*	*Date of Independence*
Anguilla	91	6,500 (78)	UK	English	-
Antigua	280	77,684 (87)	Ind.	English	1981
Aruba	193	65,000 (87)	Neth.	Dutch[b]	-
Bahamas	13,935	240,000 (87)	Ind.	English	1973
Barbados	430	286,491 (86)	Ind.	English	1966
Barbuda	16	11,585 (87)	Antigua	English	1981
Belize	22,963	171,000 (86)	Ind.	English	1981
Bequia	18	n/a	St.Vinc.	English	1979
Bermuda	54	57,000 (87)	UK	English	-
Bonaire	288	n/a[a]	Neth.	Dutch	-
Carriacou	29	n/a	Grenada	English	1974
Cayman Is.	260	22,000 (87)	UK	English	-
Cuba	114,478	10,200,000 (87)[a]	Ind.	Spanish	1898
Curazao	444	184,000 (87)	Neth.	Dutch[b]	-
Dominica	753	83,000 (87)	Ind.	English	1979
Dominican Rep.	48,442	64,16,000 (86)	Ind.	Spanish	1844
French Guiana	90,909	82,000 (86)	France	French	-
Granada	344	110,000 (87)	Ind.	English	1974
Grenadines[c]	78	6,000 (87)	St.Vinc.	English	1979
Guadeloupe	1,372	334,519 (87)	France	French	-
Guyana	214,970	800,000 (est)	Ind.	English	1966
Haiti	24,749	5,500,000 (87)	Ind.	French[b]	1804
Jamaica	10,991	2,325,500 (87)	Ind.	English	1962
Martinique	1,080	333,275 (87)	France	French	-
Montserrat	102	12,500 (87)	UK	English	-
Nevis	93	9,300 (87)	St.Kitts	English	1983
Puerto Rico	8,897	3,404,000 (87)	USA	Spanish	-
Saba	13	n/a	NA	Dutch	-
St.Barthelemy	n/a	3,500 (87)	Guadeloupe	French	-
St.Eustatius	21	n/a	NA	Dutch	-
St.Kitts	176	35,000 (87)	Ind.	English	1983
St.Lucia	616	130,000 (87)	Ind.	English	1979
St.Martin	34	30,800 (87)	Guad/NA	Fr./Dutch	-
St.Vincent	389	104,000 (87)	Ind.	English	1979
Suriname	163,265	400,000 (est)	Ind.	Dutch[b]	1975
Tobago	300	n/a	Trinidad	English	1962
Trinidad	4,828	1,217,000 (87)	Ind.	English	1962
Turks/Caicos	430	9,500 (87)	UK	English	-
Virgin Is.[d]	174	12,017 (87)	UK	English	-
Virgin Is.[e]	354	110,800 (87)	USA	English	-

Sources: Based on figures in *Latin American and Caribbean Review,* World of Information, Essex, 1988, and *The Caribbean Handbook 1988,* FT Caribbean, Antigua.

Notes: [a]Figures for the Federation of the Netherland Antilles, whose administrative center is Curazao. [b]Also Creole (Haiti), Papiamento (NA) and Sranang Tongo (Suriname). [c]Includes Mayreau, Camonan, and Union Is. [d]Includes Anegada, Tortola, and Virgin Gorda. [e]Includes St. Croix, St.Thomas, and St. John.

of petroleum by-products—two resources that are economically and strategically vital to the United States—also come from the Caribbean.[4] In addition, there are a number of oil refineries in the area, as well as reserves of other less strategic resources, such as nickel, cobalt, and gold.

In peacetime, 44 percent of total foreign cargo and 45 percent of all crude oil imports to the United States cross the Caribbean. In wartime, it is assumed that 50 percent of NATO supplies would cross the Caribbean Basin; U.S. troop reinforcements would also depart from Gulf ports en route to Europe.[5]

Consequently, from the strategic point of view, freedom of movement within the Caribbean Basin is an essential factor for U.S. security. The United States must guarantee access to the region's raw materials, trade, investment opportunities, and transport routes in order to protect the U.S. southern flank and communications with its North Atlantic allies.[6]

A second definition, adhering to political economics and a Third World perspective, seeks to group together all developing countries washed by the Caribbean, clearly distinguishing them from the industrialized North, which it automatically excludes from the region. Needless to say, this definition aims at joint action by the non-Hispanic Caribbean states and the Latin American states, based on coordinated positions in regard to the establishment of a New International Economic Order, South-South cooperation, North-South dialogue, and regional economic organizations such as the Latin American Economic System (SELA).[7]

Finally, the third definition restricts the Caribbean region to its island states, Belize, and the three Guianas—that is to say, the *West Indies*—based on the shared ethnohistorical experience of the plantation economy and slavery, including the introduction into the area of large contingents of African slave populations, from which the region's present Afro-Caribbean identity is derived. In this context and from the point of view of regional dynamics, the CARICOM states are the leading actors. This definition stresses the identity of the island Caribbean, based not only on common ethnohistorical elements but on shared aspirations regarding economic development and political evolution that contrast with those of both North America and Latin America.[8]

Each of these three definitions reflects a separate set of realities and aspirations. For example, the geostrategic definition is linked to the U.S. aspiration to turn the Caribbean Basin into an "American lake," in order to guarantee security along the U.S. southern flank in the event of East-West confrontation. As such, it redefines U.S. policy toward the hemisphere, abandoning the "Latin American" approach—followed throughout the whole of this century—in favor of a subregional, or "Caribbean," policy that is more in line with new U.S. foreign policy objectives and readjustments in the global framework.

The Third World approach reflects aspirations typical of the 1970s, whereby developing countries would gain autonomy as part of the Third World—specifically, Latin America and the Caribbean converging to face the industrialized world. During the 1980s, however, this view clashed with the reality of clearly contrasting expectations as to relations with the industrialized world and policies for insertion in the international system. For example, the Latin American perception that the non-Hispanic Caribbean enjoys a privileged relationship with the United States, the EEC, and Canada—through the Caribbean Basin Initiative, Lomé, and Caribcan—continues to clash with the reciprocal Caribbean view that Spanish-speaking Latin American nations systematically ignore the non-Hispanic Caribbean in international negotiations and that the Caribbean is becoming increasingly marginal to the powerful industrialized West. The impact of such differences on relations between the two groups of countries was evidenced when Argentine Foreign Minister Dante Caputo and Barbadian Ambassador Nita Barrow competed for the Latin American/Caribbean candidature for chairman of the 1988 UN General Assembly.[9]

The ethnohistorical definition reflects a strictly regional view, falling clearly within boundaries established by ethnohistorical and sociopolitical elements. It is based on a persisting Afro-Caribbean bias, allowing for economic and strategic ties to the industrialized West while maintaining historical and cultural ties to Africa. Efforts to set up an economic integration and cooperation scheme based on this approach have not been successful. Significantly, however, the convergence of views attained by the Caribbean states in international forums has been exceptional and has given the region's actors an important role in the international system despite its limited size, population, and economic potential.

All three definitions became highly relevant—and were challenged—in the 1970s, when substantial changes began to take place in the international system. Together with the controversial decline in hegemony of the United States, numerous centers of international influence began to crop up, replacing the postwar bipolar model and U.S. global economic and political hegemony.

In this context, the United States developed a two-pronged policy. On the one hand, its global policy was restructured to adjust to new objectives vis-à-vis Europe and Japan, seeking to strengthen the efficiency of the capitalist group of countries, while the Soviet Union and China were dealt with so as to intensify the differences between them to the advantage of the United States. This policy was implemented during President Nixon's visit to China and it was furthered by détente and a thawing of relations with the Eastern bloc.

On the other hand, changes in the balance of power among industrialized countries led to increasing coordination among less powerful nations, through initiatives such as the Group of 77 and the Movement of Non-Aligned Countries (NAM). These forums rejected the existence of political blocs, criticized the role of foreign investment and multinationals, questioned the bias of existing military alliances and treaties, and sought to establish a New International Economic Order (NIEO).

Faced with this scenario, the United States set in motion a new global policy whereby it would deal individually with Third World countries, classifying them according to their economic and strategic importance in relation to U.S. priorities, rather than by geographic location. This new policy, implemented during the 1970s, emphasized the so-called "emerging" or "regional" powers (beginning with Mexico and Brazil) and established priorities according to countries and issues, to the detriment of the traditional geographic approach.

This new Third World approach undermined the former regional policy that had shaped U.S. foreign policy in preceding decades and served as a framework for a "Latin American policy," which had been developed through the inter-American system and the OAS.

Indeed, the "Latin America" category to which U.S. policy had attached great importance in previous years was displaced by a new global view toward the developing world. U.S. activity was restructured according to political criteria, such as military cooperation, foreign investment, transfer of technology, trade, and overseas development aid—criteria that were applied to countries according to their stage of development and geostrategic importance, regardless of their specific geographical location.[10]

The Caribbean Basin Initiative was designed within the framework of this new policy, which was formulated during the Carter administration and implemented by the Reagan administration. Reagan's new geopolitical global view replaced the previous administration's moralistic or economic bias. The CBI was set in the context of a geostrategic perception of the Caribbean subregion as defined basically by three critical endogenous processes: first, the Cuban revolution and its consolidation; second, the political independence of former British and Dutch colonies; and third, the growing Central American crisis.

Ray Cline's geopolitical views, which influenced U.S. decisionmakers in the early 1980s, took even further this definition of the Caribbean subregion as an entity separate from Latin America by conceiving a view of the United States as the center of an area spanning Alaska to the Caribbean Sea and viewing Canada, Mexico, Central America, and the island Caribbean all as part of a "North American territory."[11] The Caribbean Basin thus became a key political and strategic area—the "fourth frontier" or southern flank. The CBI was perceived both in terms of obvious strategic considerations and as part of a policy to promote the region's progressive economic incorporation into the North American conglomerate.

The intensification of the Central American crisis led to another subdivision of the Caribbean Basin from the U.S. point of view, which came to regard Central America as a direct threat to its interests (particularly in the Panama Canal zone) and to regard the island Caribbean only as a potential threat,[12] in view of its political stability and the conservative and pragmatic position held by most non-Hispanic Caribbean postcolonial governments.

This differentiation on the part of the United States strengthened the position of some non-Hispanic Caribbean leaders that the region's own dynamics are based on distinct ethnohistorical features and sociopolitical similarities, a perception that CARICOM member states were to promote strongly. The recent decolonization process, the attempt to form a West Indian federation, shared membership in the British Commonwealth, and comparable cultural and political characteristics contributed toward the perception of a common identity in a hemispheric and world context.

Differentiation from momentarily unstable Central America, and from the potentially threatening middle powers in the region such as Venezuela, Mexico, or Cuba, seemed to justify limiting the region to the West Indies. Thus Suriname, Haiti, and the Dominican Republic have remained in limbo as CARICOM "observers" and regional integration efforts exclude participation by Latin America. Simultaneously, the English-speaking Caribbean states have achieved greater autonomy in their foreign policies, with strong regional emphasis and a nonaligned stance at the international level.

On the other hand, the growing influence of Third World countries, both through participation in international forums and because of the increased pressure and coordination achieved by raw material producers—i.e., oil producers within OPEC or, on a lesser scale, bauxite producers within the IBA—has contributed to the perception of a homogeneous and united Third World, confronted by the industrialized North.

Promotion of the New International Economic Order and of South-South cooperation, as well as defense of the interests of developing countries by Caribbean Basin states, has led to a stronger perception of the subregion as a homogeneous part of the Third World, particularly in the wake of actions of regional leaders such as Michael Manley, Carlos Andrés Pérez, and Luis Echeverría and the creation of organizations such as SELA. These instances of cooperation have led, moreover, to various types of socialist experiments, particularly in the non-Hispanic Caribbean, i.e., Jamaica, Guyana, Grenada, and Suriname, which were linked to the more radical Cuban and Nicaraguan processes.

In addition to these developments, during the 1970s the area was for the first time witness to repeated cooperative efforts and agreements that transcended SELA and included the establishment of regional mechanisms such as NAMUCAR, GEPLACEA, and others. Latin American states, among them Mexico, Venezuela, Cuba, and Colombia, took their first steps in this direction too with the development of Third World-oriented "Caribbean" policies that prevailed, despite ups and downs, throughout the 1970s and early 1980s.

It is no coincidence that this process was intended to offset diplomatic pressure by Southern Cone military regimes, particularly on Cuba and on Latin American democracies in the Caribbean Basin, which were eager to form new alliances and needed to expand their support in the hemisphere.[13]

Consistently decreasing international oil and bauxite prices and growing external debt proved, however, that Third World harmony would have a short life, when faced with economic action by the industrialized North. At political, ideological, and military levels, U.S. intervention in Grenada and the Malvinas war were clear illustrations of the inadequacy of the inter-American security system as to any regional initiative that could affect U.S. global policy. Both crises served to intensify the traditional dividing lines between Latin America and the non-Hispanic Caribbean, owing to alignments during the South Atlantic war and the notorious inability of the OAS and of Latin America to react during the Grenadan crisis.

The external debt problem, in turn, highlighted the hemisphere's difficulties in producing a coordinated economic effort, despite the political cohesion demonstrated by the Contadora Group in regard to the Central American conflicts and, more recently, by the Group of Eight.

The three predominant definitions of the Caribbean lead to a clear differentiation of three sets of regional actors. First, there are those regional actors who fit the West Indian definition and are geographically linked to the Caribbean Sea. Notwithstanding their ethnohistorical similarities, these actors are clearly differentiated by culture and language and by their place within the international system. Prominent among them are the CARICOM member states and Cuba, which exercise significant leadership in international forums and organizations. Cuba, however, is often considered in its own category as a regional power whose foreign policy has considerable weight. Other autonomous regional actors are the Dominican Republic, Suriname, and Haiti, all of which have waited for over a decade for accession to CARICOM. Aruba and the Federation of the Netherlands Antilles, despite their links with Holland, also aspire to future membership.

Second, in addition to regional players, extraregional actors notably affect the geopolitical dynamics of the region. Foremost among them are the United States and its North Atlantic allies with historical ties to the Caribbean, such as Great Britain, France, and to a somewhat lesser degree, Holland and Canada. The Soviet Union also belongs in this grouping, by virtue of its relations with Cuba and within the framework of the East-West conflict. Lastly, Puerto Rico plays a very specific role in U.S. regional strategy.

Third, the Caribbean presence of the Latin American middle powers has increased since the 1970s, despite their apparently marginal role. Mexico, Venezuela, Colombia, and Brazil today possess relatively close geographical, economic, and political links with the region.

All of these actors affect the island Caribbean geopolitical dynamics to a greater or lesser extent and will play a determining role whenever measures to guarantee regional security and peace are needed.

The Caribbean: Distinct Characteristics

Notwithstanding the common ethnohistorical attributes of West Indian societies, profound linguistic, cultural, political, social, and economic differences exist to divide them. Although most of them have undergone a colonization process characterized by the development of a plantation economy and the exploitation of African slave labor, the differences in policy and style among the several occupying powers during the colonial period have left their mark.

Since the sale of the Virgin Islands by Denmark to the United States in 1917, the non-Hispanic Caribbean has been composed of four major zones of metropolitan influence: (1) the former British colonies and territories still under British rule; (2) Suriname, which gained its independence from Holland in 1975, and the Netherlands Antilles and Aruba, associated Dutch states; (3) the French Overseas Departments (DOM) and Haiti, which became independent from France in 1804; and (4) the associated states of the United States. This first classification of the region in terms of colonial and neocolonial links allows for a fifth sphere with Latin American ties—i.e., Cuba and the Dominican Republic, which have traditionally been associated with the continent, although their political independence was gained in the late nineteenth century. Haiti is an atypical case. It gained independence from France in the early nineteenth century, when a successful uprising of slaves brought into being the first black state in the region. This turn of events, together with the distinct French influence upon Haitian culture and institutions and its early participation in the inter-American system, have frequently led to the inclusion of Haiti in the Latin American conglomerate.[14]

Another atypical case in the region is Puerto Rico, which was originally a Spanish colony. Though it is now associated with the United States, its Hispanic and Latin American identity definitely persists.

Moreover, the areas under European and U.S. colonial and neocolonial influence have not shown uniform signs of colonization; they were subject, instead, to the impact of colonial power conflicts beginning in the sixteenth century and to successive transfers of colonial control, resulting in a disorderly and still persisting mix of linguistic, cultural, institutional, and racial characteristics.[15]

While the societies subject to European and U.S. influence experienced various modalities of colonial dependency and currently are characterized by diverse forms of political organization, the group historically under British colonial rule is at least equally complex. This group, composed of a total of sixteen island territories and two continental territories, displays a wide range of economic, political, social, and ethnocultural diversity, while also showing marked differences in population, degree of economic development and potential, and degree to which they are linked to the metropolitan centers.

After a fruitless attempt to form a West Indies Federation—which lasted from 1958 to 1962—the first territories to gain their political independence from Great Britain were Jamaica and Trinidad, in 1962. They were followed by Guyana and Barbados in 1966. Significantly, these are the four most populated states of the former British colonies, with the highest degree of economic development and infrastructure. Moreover, the first three are rich in mineral resources (bauxite, petroleum) and Barbados has a thriving tourist industry. These four states are known as the English-speaking Caribbean's More Developed Countries (MDCs).

Subsequently, beginning in 1973, independence was gained by the Bahamas, followed by Grenada (1974), Dominica, St. Vincent, and St. Lucia (1979), Antigua and Belize (1981), and St. Kitts-Nevis (1983). With the exception of Belize, these were island territories frequently besieged by attempts to secede on the part of the lesser islands formally associated with them in the independence process. Substantially less populated than the four larger states, these territories are also markedly less developed and highly dependent upon agricultural production and upon exports both to the British market and, through the Lomé III agreement, to the European Economic Community.[16] These countries are therefore generally referred to as the Less Developed Countries (LDCs).

While the bulk of MDC trade is with the United States,[17] the English-speaking Caribbean LDCs export mostly to the United Kingdom and the EEC and enjoy, even today, a considerable amount of British economic assistance.[18]

Finally, there are six territories that are still British associated states, all highly dependent upon British aid.[19] These territories, each of which has a population under 60,000 and is characterized by limited economic development, are Anguilla, Bermuda, the British Virgin Islands, the Cayman Islands, Montserrat, and the Turks and Caicos Islands.

The institutional dependence of these territories and states upon Great Britain is evidenced by the persistence of parliamentary systems based on the Westminster model.[20] Furthermore, the independent English-speaking Caribbean states have remained members of the British Commonwealth of Nations, which recognizes the British Crown as the association's symbol and whose principal function is to provide economic assistance to its member states, as well as diplomatic support, particularly for the smaller states.

Continued ties with the United Kingdom can be more fully understood if we recall the nature of the political independence processes of these states, which were conducted within the so-called constitutional decolonization process that took place after World War II and involved no national liberation struggles. Historically, therefore, the identity of these states has been strongly linked to their cultural, economic, and political ties to Great Britain.

The former Dutch colonial territories include Suriname, which, since achieving independence in 1975, has also maintained a parliamentary system (with the exception of the period 1980–1987 when it was ruled by a military regime) and a federation of the Netherlands Antilles, which exists as an associated state of the Kingdom of the Netherlands. However, in recent years, tensions have arisen between Aruba and the remaining territories of this federation—Curazao, Bonaire, Saba, St. Eustatius, and St. Maarten—leading to the establishment of separate ties between Aruba and the Netherlands until the former's political independence is finalized in 1996.[21]

Aruba's economic situation and that of the Netherlands Antilles have been affected by the closing of the petroleum refinery in Aruba and by Shell's decision to close a similar refinery in Curazao—which was finally purchased by Venezuela after heavy negotiation among Shell, Holland, and Venezuela. At present, the bulk of these islands' local income is derived from tourism. Nevertheless, these island territories are privileged in that most of their GNP is obtained from Dutch economic assistance, despite the fact that the Netherlands are promoting their independence.[22]

Dutch investments in the region are generally limited and are channeled through two Dutch corporations: Heineken, which influences the entire region, and Royal Dutch Shell, whose influence has notably diminished since the transfer of its Curazao refinery.

The Surinamese economic situation, in turn, deteriorated considerably during the period of the military government, partially because of the suspension of Dutch economic assistance and the fall in the international price of bauxite, the country's main export product.[23]

Since 1946, Martinique, French Guiana, and Guadeloupe—the latter including the two subordinate territories of St. Barthelemy and St. Martin (which it shares with the Netherlands)—have held special status among the French Overseas Departments (DOM). Politically, these departments are an integral part of France and have their own representatives in the National Assembly and the Senate. France, in turn, designates a prefect for each department, although in recent years there has been an increasing tendency toward decentralization. In general, these territories have achieved a very limited degree of industrialization. U.S. investments have been noticeably absent; thus, they are highly dependent upon French economic assistance and trade in order to maintain their relatively high standard of living as compared to the rest of the Caribbean.[24]

Puerto Rico and the U.S. Virgin Islands possess associate state status with the United States. In 1917, Puerto Ricans were granted U.S. citizenship and in 1952, Puerto Rico became the *Commonwealth of Puerto Rico* or Estado Libre Asociado, with a degree of self-government. Beginning in the late 1940s, this island developed an industrialization strategy called Operation Bootstrap, which was based on fiscal incentives for U.S. investment and which has been a model for the rest of the island Caribbean.While this strategy contributed to highly dependent development, since numerous U.S. companies settled on the island to produce for the U.S. market, it also contributed toward making Puerto Rico one of the states with the highest per capita income in the region, through substantial U.S. funding for social programs, particularly food subsidies for wide sectors of the population. However, in recent years, unemployment has risen significantly and over 2 million Puerto Ricans have emigrated to the United States, out of a total present population of 3.2 million.[25]

At present, U.S. companies control the Puerto Rican economy, to the extent that the Department of Commerce reports that 90 percent of new industrial investments have been financed by companies from the continental United States.[26] The situation is the same in the U.S. Virgin Islands, where U.S. companies control all economic sectors—petroleum refining, construction, tourism, and trade.

Since the 1950s Puerto Rico, particularly, has served as a model for the so-called "industrialization by invitation" strategy, which, especially during the following decade, was imitated by the English-speaking Caribbean MDCs. Some of its economic formulas began making a second appearance during the 1980s, with the launching of the Caribbean Basin Initiative (CBI).

In view of the advantages to be gained from continued economic assistance, dependent territories tend to maintain their links with their respective metropolitan centers, despite the reluctance of some of the latter. Because of this, the political, institutional, and economic situation in the non-Hispanic Caribbean is undergoing a general reversal of the decolonization process that was typical of the region in the 1960s and 1970s. This has also resulted in attendant socioeconomic, political, and cultural consequences. The situation is not entirely unrelated to the economic and political frustrations that arose in the wake of some of the development strategies implemented during the postcolonial period in most of the independent states.

Economic Development Strategies

One of the foremost promoters of the "industrialization by invitation" strategy developed in the English-speaking Caribbean in the 1950s was the St. Lucian economist Arthur Lewis, who agreed with some of the ECLAC ideas of the time, emphasizing industrialization and economic diversification as the paths along which economic development should be guided.[27] Arthur Lewis proposed an industrialization strategy based on foreign capital investments as an alternative to development based principally on agricultural exports. This strategy, aimed at replacing the plantation economy and at overcoming the increasing unemployment it had generated, was set in a framework of dependent development, inspired by the post–World War II Puerto Rican experience.[28]

Seen from this perspective, the principal objective of the proposal was to attract foreign private investment, especially in the export-oriented manufacturing sector, by offering tax rebates and low wages. The aims were primarily to promote the manufacturing industry and, to a lesser extent, to make agriculture more productive. Basically, this strategy relied on the creation of state incentives for establishing transnational enterprises in English-speaking Caribbean territories; the creation of a "truce" atmosphere between industry and labor to guarantee the security of investment; progressive development of an adequate infrastructure by the state; less emphasis on agriculture, the mainstay of the colonial plantation economy; and promotion of a complementary tourist industry, to generate additional employment in the service sector and to bring about a general improvement in local human resources.[29]

From the point of view of this strategy, since the region was unable to undertake internal capitalization to sustain new industries, industrial development would require foreign capital investments that would in turn open the doors for exports to wider markets and provide managerial resources unavailable in the Caribbean. The principal incentives were the availability of abundant cheap labor in comparison with other regions and the existence of a stable political and labor climate. This strategy assigned an active role to the state—requiring it to implement agrarian reform, to develop roadways and infrastructures, and to offer incentives to attract foreign investors, while also expecting it to correct any imbalances that might occur in the long run as a result of foreign investment in specific economic sectors.[30]

Many governments in the non-Hispanic Caribbean adopted this strategy, establishing industrial development companies along the lines of the Puerto Rican experience and offering fiscal incentives clearly aimed at attracting foreign investments. They did not, however, create a regional economic integration base to support the process, as was later proposed by William Demas, who deemed such a base indispensable for any development strategy in the small Caribbean states.[31] "Industrialization by invitation" was openly fostered by the Four Powers Commission that emerged from the Anglo-American Caribbean Commission—originally set up by the United States and Great Britain in the early 1940s and later joined by France and Holland—with a view to adopting a regional approach to basic cooperation problems in the Caribbean at a time when the former European colonial centers were beginning their gradual withdrawal from the region.

In the 1960s, the strategy recommended by Arthur Lewis led to some economic growth in the more developed territories such as Trinidad and Jamaica, in the form of marked industrial development and an increase in per capita income.[32] Other territories, however, were not so fortunate. MDCs such as Barbados and Guyana and the Eastern Caribbean LDCs were generally unsuccessful in attracting substantial capital inflows to promote industrialization. A similar situation arose in the Dutch and French territories, which were highly dependent upon economic assistance from the metropolitan centers to sustain their relatively high standards of living.

The success of Jamaica and Trinidad with this strategy did not lead to substantial relief of the endemic unemployment and poverty in the non-Hispanic Caribbean, which became even more serious in the 1970s as a result of the agricultural crisis.[33] Instead, the strategy led generally to a succession of negative results, owing to the fact that most industries developed during this period were principally in the mining sector and were thus capital-intensive rather than labor-intensive. Moreover, they were not conducive to horizontal integration, given their dependence on external inputs and markets. This situation was compounded by social conditions derived from an increase in migration to the cities and consequent urban concentration, as well as by heightened social and political tensions caused by greater unemployment, as foreseen in the late 1960s.[34]

Some of the main reasons for the failure of this strategy can be found in the historical matrix of the plantation economy and its links with the metropolitan economies. In most island territories, income is mainly derived from agricultural products—sugar in Antigua, Nevis, St. Kitts, Montserrat, and Anguilla; and bananas, citrus fruits, and spices in Dominica, St. Lucia, St. Vincent, and Grenada. In fact, in 1970, agriculture continued to employ 33 percent of labor in the region, with 50 percent of agricultural workers employed in growing sugar and bananas for export.[35]

Since before World War II, however, plantations in most of the territories were being taken over by foreign companies. Such was the case with Booker Bros. in Guyana and Caroni Ltd in Trinidad—both in the sugar industry and both linked to McConnell Ltd, to Tate and Lyle of Great Britain, and to Geest Industries, banana growers and traders in St. Lucia, St. Vincent, Grenada, and Dominica, currently among the largest British fruit traders. The concentration of plantation ownership in British hands led to the diversification of company activities, with investments in shipping companies, processing plants, and financing activities.[36]

In late 1967 in the English-speaking Caribbean alone, U.S. private investment stood at $1.526 billion, British investment at $637 million, and Canadian investment at $431 million, amounting to a total of $2.594 billion for the three countries. By 1971, these investments had increased to $3.785 billion.[37] The vast majority of investments were in the mining sector—particularly petroleum in Trinidad and bauxite in Jamaica and Guyana—and were made predominantly by U.S.- and Canadian-owned companies, while British investments were concentrated mainly in agriculture.[38] Significant investments were also made by metropolitan corporations in the trade, shipping, and financial sectors.[39]

U.S. interests displaced British interests significantly in the 1960s,[40] when U.S. investment increased drastically in comparison with British investment.[41] Displacement of British and Dutch economic interests had begun, however, during the period following World War II. Transfer of British military bases in the Caribbean to the United States during the war greatly increased U.S. strategic presence in the area.

Meanwhile, migration of youth to the cities greatly increased, owing to several converging factors—agricultural mechanization, a restricted labor market and fall in agricultural prices, the hope for better jobs and salaries in urban centers, as well as psychological and cultural factors, which kept rural young people from seeking employment on the plantations. The young urban population, however, which was predominantly black and unemployed or underemployed, remained unaffected by the industrialization process and educational advances made in more developed Caribbean societies.

Furthermore, during the postwar decades the patronizing nature of the political system was undergoing a process of gradual decolonization. Yet, the political elite that made its appearance during this process in the English- and Dutch-speaking Caribbean saw its political power threatened because, despite having attained control of the state, it was ostracized by the multinational corporations in control of the economy and suffered the consequences of the "industrialization by invitation" strategy. Concurrently, a young intelligentsia with its own power ambitions began to take form, set apart by a generation gap from the local elite that represented the postcolonial political system. This new intelligentsia agreed ideologically with some sectors of the elite in its growing concern about their shared distance from and lack of control over production.

These circumstances, taken together, created the conditions for the ideological takeover of English- and Dutch-speaking Caribbean societies by a particularly radical nationalism rooted in Black Power ideas. They also resulted in the deployment of new development strategies that fell generally within the area of a "noncapitalist path of development." It should be noted, however, that the Cuban influence in this process was actually very limited.[42]

During the 1970s, an appropriate climate arose for governmental experiments with explicit socialist positions. Among the contibuting factors were increasing internal political and social tensions dating from the previous decade and certain specific changes in the international scene—particularly changes in U.S. foreign policy introduced by the Carter administration, and the new Cuban regional policy.

In the early 1970s state participation in the national economy increased in some countries as a result of greater interest by the political elite in achieving control of economic resources in their respective countries and the tendency to implement economic, social, and political development models with distinct nationalistic features. This was particularly true of Guyana, Jamaica, and Grenada, where development strategies based on greater state participation were implemented when socialist-oriented parties rose to power. This process also included Trinidad to some extent, where the People's National Movement—despite its explicit identification with a capitalist model favoring free enterprise and investment by multinational corporations—increased government control of various economic sectors after the political crises of 1970 and 1975.[43] In Suriname as well, the 1980 takeover by a military regime following the "revolution of the sergeants" led, albeit haltingly, to political measures put forward as conducive to socialist transformation in the former Dutch colony.[44]

A nationalistic and socialistic bias was particularly evident in Jamaica from 1976 to 1980 under the People's National Party, when the state increased its control over bauxite production and processing, beginning in 1974, in the context of "democratic socialism." The process was even more marked in Guyana, under the government of the People's National Congress, where nationalization of the principal economic sectors (bauxite and sugar) began in 1973. Here the ruling party became identified with "cooperative socialism," strongly inspired by the Tanzanian experience. The effort of these governments to implement trisectoral economies, stimulating the development of a cooperative sector and increasing state participation in the mining industry, generated an open debate in the region on taking a "noncapitalist path" toward development. This effort reached a high point in Grenada between 1979 and 1983, with the rise to power of a socialist government, which put into practice many of the proposals previously made by the Caribbean intelligentsia during the emergence of the Black Power movement, and which also attempted to implement some of the ideas of the New World Group.[45]

In Grenada this process was accompanied by an attempt to develop an economic diversification strategy in agricultural production, a strategy that included agrarian reform and agro-industrial projects, without, however, affecting foreign investment in tourism and banking. The process was interrupted, principally because of internal conflict between rival political factions and because of U.S. intervention. U.S. action also affected the contradictory and limited socialist progress made in Suriname, where geopolitical pressures were applied beginning in October 1983.

Attempts at Regional Economic Integration and Cooperation

Historically, the difficulties inherent in the colonial administration of the tiny and dispersed Caribbean islands led to repeated attempts by the British government to form regional federations, particularly in the Eastern Caribbean. The attempt to form a West Indies Federation in 1958 had thus been preceded by a number of cooperative experiments in the English-speaking islands, among them a federation of the Leeward Islands in 1674 and a more formal initiative to create a Common Council in 1871. All of these efforts were partial endeavors at legislative and administrative integration, with a view to facilitating government in Eastern Caribbean island territories.

The fact that British continental and island territories were geographically isolated from each other, as well as hindered by unfavorable tides and winds in their attempts to establish a functional communications network, worked strongly against the success of these efforts at integration. However, after World War II, regular air traffic was established among the scattered English-speaking Caribbean territories.

The idea of a federation had been repeatedly proposed by the various royal commissions that had visited the region since the late nineteenth century. During the postwar period, it found a strong echo among labor unions, political parties, and business groups, which were beginning to advocate greater autonomy and, in the long run, political independence.

The rise of the nationalist movement across the English-speaking Caribbean during the 1940s and 1950s first sparked the aspirations of the several political elites to form a regional federation that would include territories as distant from each other as Jamaica and Guyana. Arguments in favor of a federation were mainly political in nature, with the possibility of achieving self-government foremost among them. It was felt that successful self-government could be facilitated by a more efficient administrative system, with a broader electorate to ensure a more stable and developed democracy, a wider scope for political action by the emerging elite, and greater possibilities for implementing the appropriate policies to remedy the region's social ills. To these political arguments was added a list of economic justifications, centering around the formation of an expanded regional market, which would also stimulate economic development both in the area as a whole and in its units, through various forms of cooperation and integration.[46] Moreover, from the ideological point of view, the political elite involved in the process envisioned a federation that would serve as a nucleus for consolidating national sentiments to oppose any extraregional agents threatening the independent survival of the units and would serve as an entity with greater bargaining power in the framework of the international system.

In January 1958, with the prior formal acceptance of the Federal Constitution proposed in 1956, the Federation of the West Indies was founded, with the exclusion of the Bahamas, British Honduras, and Guyana. The federation was conceived as a colonial federal entity, with a governor-general appointed by Great Britain and a legislature comprised of a senate of 19 appointed members and a house of representatives with 45 members to be elected by universal adult vote. Seventeen of these benches were assigned to Jamaica, 10 to Trinidad, 5 to Barbados, and 2 each to the remaining territories, with the exception of Montserrat, which had only one bench. Instead of a cabinet, a council of state was formed, presided over by the governor and organized by a prime minister, who was elected by a majority vote. Thus, the federation included ten British colonies in the region, which at the time represented a total of 3 million inhabitants, distributed among Antigua (with Redonda and Barbuda included as administrative units), Barbados, Dominica,

Grenada, Jamaica (including the Cayman Islands), Montserrat, St. Kitts-Nevis-Anguilla, St. Lucia, St. Vincent (including the Grenadines), and Trinidad and Tobago.

However, there were obvious differences among the members of the federation in terms of territorial and demographic size, not unrelated to marked differences in economic development and political autonomy.[47] Moreover, by 1958, Barbados, Jamaica, and Trinidad had already achieved partial autonomy and self-government and therefore, for them, joining the federation meant taking a step backward politically.[48]

In practice, the more enthusiastic partisans of federation were the smaller territories, where federation seemed to promise speedier access to political independence. However, imbalances in political representation and financial contributions by the smaller and larger states were compounded with the contradictions arising from island vs. federal interests, all of which factors contributed significantly to the federation's collapse in 1962, just four years after its founding. This set a precedent for persisting tension between the smaller islands and the more developed territories in the English-speaking Caribbean. This tension was fueled even further in later years by another fruitless attempt—a federation of Eastern Caribbean territories, including Barbados, which fell apart when the latter withdrew.

In summary, owing to limited participation by the masses in stimulating and promoting the idea of federation, the lack of dissemination of this idea by organizations other than the ruling political parties, and marked ideological dependence of the political elite on Great Britain, which was applying moderate pressure in the matter, the federation concept was unable to surmount the inevitable obstacles posed by deeply rooted island loyalties and local chauvinisms.

The Federation of the Netherlands Antilles, though longer-lasting and more stable, underwent a similar process. It was founded in 1954 within the framework of the Tripartite Kingdom of the Netherlands, Suriname, and the Netherlands Antilles, after the dismantling of the Dutch colonial system was initiated by the independence struggle of Indonesia. The creation of the Tripartite Kingdom granted a measure of autonomy to the Caribbean territories, as one way of evading United Nations supervision of colonial systems. In 1975, Suriname achieved independence and withdrew from the scheme. Recent tensions between Aruba and Curazao and the reluctance of the former to contribute economically to the federation have led Aruba to separate from it as well and to set up direct links with Holland. Certain sectors in St. Maarten are also seeking independence from the federation, particularly in view of high maintenance costs for the islands of Saba, St. Eustatius, and Bonaire, whose limited income is derived from small volumes of tourism.[49] The current trend in the Dutch territories is to strengthen ties with the Netherlands, for the sake of economic assistance.

A similar situation is found in the French DOMs, where the concept of autonomy increasingly prevails over the idea of total independence from France. Partisans of assimilation or independence are decreasing and, in fact, taking up positions gradually closer to those who favor autonomy.[50] Though characterized by its own particularities, this situation is also to be found in Puerto Rico, where partisans of autonomy predominate over those favoring commonwealth status and those favoring independence.[51]

After the foiled attempt at a West Indian political federation, the idea of regional integration gained ground as a prerequisite for economic development in the English-speaking Caribbean. Initial steps, however, were cautious. Attempts were made to advance first along the lines of economic integration, with a long-term view to eventually arrive at some form of political integration.

The first step in the direction of regional economic integration and development was taken in 1967, with the creation of the Caribbean Free Trade Association (CARIFTA). Some experts, however, questioned this initiative on the grounds that it did not provide for integration of certain key production sectors in the region.[52]

The creation of CARIFTA in the 1960s was followed by the creation of the Caribbean Community, or CARICOM, in 1973, with the express objective of furthering regional economic integration in order to promote economic development in the English-speaking Caribbean territories. From its inception, CARICOM—which includes Antigua, the Bahamas, Belize, Barbados, Dominica, Grenada, Guyana, Jamaica, Montserrat, St. Kitts-Nevis, St. Lucia, St. Vincent, and Trinidad and Tobago—has addressed three principal issues: (1) economic integration, in terms of both free trade and production; (2) functional cooperation in various areas; and (3) foreign policy coordination.

In the first area, particularly, existing regional contradictions between national interests and regional objectives have come to the fore, primarily with respect to intraregional trade. Although intraregional trade grew during the 1970s, exchange restrictions in place in Jamaica and Guyana and the diminished availability of foreign currency there caused significant deterioration by the end of the decade, when heavy restrictions were imposed on regional trade.[53] In addition to these restrictions, the lack of coordination in the CARICOM member states' production activities led also to product duplication. A regional economic crisis resulted, with particular consequences for the LDCs, which were dependent upon agricultural products and affected by the world recession as well. The LDCs were forced to form a subgroup within CARICOM, the Organization of Eastern Caribbean States (OECS), established in 1981 to deal with their specific problems.

CARICOM has been more successful in its efforts to coordinate educational, transportation, health, and technical assistance policies. Nevertheless, conflicting interests between the MDCs and the LDCs have caused similar problems in this area, particularly in relation to financing the University of the West Indies (whose campuses are located in Jamaica, Barbados, and Trinidad) and in regard to the creation of a regional airline.[54] The lack of popular participation in these policies has also been repeatedly criticized.[55]

Foreign policy coordination, the third area provided for in the Chaguaramas Treaty establishing CARICOM, has also been adversely affected in recent years. Coordination has generally been effective in regard to economic and political topics, such as participation within the ACP grouping, and in the United Nations and OAS; and in relation to specific matters such as diplomatic relations with Cuba, the Panama Canal, the Law of the Sea, and Guyana and Belize's territorial conflicts with Venezuela and Guatemala, respectively. However, some analysts point out that the international bargaining potential of such coordination has not been fully utilized,[56] but has, instead, been seriously hampered by the tendency to enter into bilateral relations, thus working against CARICOM joint action. In relation to the Caribbean Basin Initiative, CARICOM has repeatedly criticized its preference for bilateral negotiations, to the detriment of multilateral agreements.

The treaty establishing the OECS in 1981, in turn, set out as its main objectives the promotion of subregional cooperation, economic integration, unity and solidarity among member states—including the defense of their sovereignty, territorial integrity, and political independence—and foreign policy coordination in defense of their common interests. At the economic level, this organizational structure has not only tended to stimulate regional trade, but has also promoted foreign investments, with a view to contributing to the economic development of these island economies, wholly dependent upon tourism and agriculture (bananas, sugarcane, cocoa, and nutmeg). Despite the increase in U.S. economic involvement, trade in agricultural products is controlled primarily by Geest, a British corporation that exports to Europe, in compliance with the Lomé agreements. In Antigua and Barbados, tourism has become the main source of foreign currency earnings, while the CBI and the economic assistance of U.S. agencies have turned light industry into an important sector in the local economies, a process facilitated by the low cost of labor in assembly industries such as electronics, textiles, and toys.

At the political level, OECS member countries have tended to harmonize their joint efforts in the foreign policy, defense, and subregional security areas. Their recent political evolution was marked by their participation in the U.S. invasion of Grenada in October 1983.

All of the above notwithstanding, the Eighth Summit Conference of CARICOM Heads of Government, held in St. Lucia on 3 July 1987, fostered optimism in regard to renewed options for regional integration. The respective CARICOM heads of government agreed to eliminate, in the near future, all measures restricting intraregional trade. This decision was taken at a time when, according to 1986 figures, intraregional trade in the English-speaking Caribbean had been reduced by 30 percent from 1981 levels, while intraregional imports had diminished by 50 percent. This deterioration was accompanied by the shutdown of local industries and by a marked increase in unemployment throughout the region.[57]

The new optimism that reigned in some Caribbean circles was apparently justified by additional measures agreed upon during the summit, such as the creation of the CARICOM Enterprise Regime and the Caribbean Export Bank, both aimed at promoting integration of the private and public sectors in the production of export goods.[58]

These measures for promoting economic development and integration addressed one of the principal concerns of the meeting—the growing external debt, which particularly affected the English-speaking MDCs. Indeed, for Jamaica, Guyana, and Trinidad and Tobago, the external debt had become a key problem, comparable in degree to that of the Latin American debtor countries.

Within the context of the OECS member states, a proposal has been put forth to advance toward political integration on the basis of the progress achieved in economic integration. Though in line with the goals of many Eastern Caribbean sectors, this proposal has met with criticism.[59]

The first observation generally made is that it was put forward unilaterally by the respective governments without prior popular consultation. Moreover, political leaders in the region evidently hold diverging views in relation to the proposal. While John Compton and James Mitchell, prime ministers of St. Lucia and St. Vincent, respectively, are promoting the initiative, the prime minister of Antigua, Vere C. Bird, has rejected it on the grounds that his country will not relinquish, for a fictitious subregional political union, the independence gained at great expense.[60]

Thus, despite initial enthusiasm, the prospects of a political union in the Eastern Caribbean are once more vanishing, and the viability of regional political integration schemes, first attempted during formation of the Federation of the West Indies, is once more being questioned.

European Community, U. S., and Canadian Assistance

In addition to regional cooperation and integration efforts mainly directed toward stimulating economic development in the region, numerous assistance and cooperation mechanisms have been designed and promoted from outside the area. Agreements have been made with Great Britain, with the United States, and with Canada, in line with the fact that, in spite of its relative geographic proximity to Latin America, the non-Hispanic Caribbean tends to establish trade links and migration processes predominantly with Europe and North America.[61]

Although Great Britain began to withdraw from the region after World War II, specific British corporate interests have justified economic assistance even in areas outside the associated territories. In particular, mechanisms created to this end were established within the framework of the various Lomé agreements entered into between the European Community and the ACP countries, all former European colonies. At present, thirteen non-Hispanic Caribbean states, including Suriname, participate in this agreement. EEC links also benefit the French overseas territories through specific assistance schemes, such as the European Regional Development Funds, the European Social Fund, and the European Fund for Agricultural Guidance and Guaranty.

The Lomé agreements provide for nonreciprocal trade benefits to participating countries through tax-free exports. Sugar exports to the EEC receive particularly preferential treatment through prices that have been set below the world market level. The Lomé III agreement also provides for an industrial cooperation program for the processing of agricultural products, a financial cooperation program for implementing development projects, and a scheme designed to compensate for fluctuations in export earnings derived from EEC trade, according to product volume (STABEX).[62] The agreement is generally seen as a form of assistance to participating countries, rather than a trade treaty per se, particularly as concerns the STABEX scheme, which combines trade and assistance and is financed from an EEC assistance fund.[63]

It should be noted that European, particularly British, economic influence in the Caribbean, albeit considerable, is totally eclipsed by U.S. interests in the area, in terms of both investment and trade. In this regard, the U.S. positive balance of trade with the region grew from $412 million in 1976 to $2.9 billion in 1982.[64]

The CBI is a U.S. assistance program expressly set up to stimulate the recovery of Caribbean Basin states affected by growing deficits in their balance of payments, increasing external debts, falling international commodity prices, diminishing investment and trade, as well as increases in their inflation and unemployment rates.[65] Initial steps in this direction were taken by the Carter administration in its efforts to implement an economic aid plan aimed at promoting U.S. investments in the Caribbean. These efforts were renewed by the Reagan administration and reformulated in the CBI.

The original concept behind an assistance program for Caribbean Basin states emerged during a meeting of Canada, Mexico, Venezuela, and the United States, held in Nassau in July 1981, to discuss a multilateral initiative. However, differences arose in relation to the political and military criteria that would guide selection of the program's beneficiary states. Although the first three countries dropped the plan, it was formalized by the United States. The launching of this initiative was reinforced by the strong emphasis placed by some regional political leaders on "the pressing need for a Caribbean assistance policy" to "cope with the explosive situation in the region," in the words of Prime Minister Edward Seaga of Jamaica during the Council of the Americas meeting of June 1981.[66]

The CBI was approved by the U.S. Congress in July 1983 and implemented in 1984, pursuant to the provisions of the Caribbean Basin Economic Recovery Act, which essentially authorized the president of the United States to allow duty-free access, during a period of twelve years, for a number of products from the beneficiary countries. In this regard, the CBI was intended to promote a specific development model, based on increased foreign private investment and export-oriented growth, stimulated by the private sector and activated by "the magic of the market," to use President Reagan's phrase. However, the Reagan administration made it quite clear from the outset that the CBI's principal objective lay in securing strategic advantages in a region shaken by political turmoil.

In line with these strategic considerations, in order to be eligible, beneficiary countries were required to: (1) not be a communist country; (2) comply with provisions relating to expropriation of property belonging to U.S. citizens; (3) take the appropriate measures to cooperate in the prevention of drug traffic to the United States; (4) recognize arbitration favorable to the United States; (5) not enter into preferential agreements with other developed countries that could adversely affect U.S. trade; (6) not disseminate materials under U.S. copyright without the consent of the owner; and (7) have entered into extradition agreements with the United States.[67]

The president of the United States was to take into account other "discretionary factors" for eligibility of a beneficiary country, among which were the willingness of the country in question to be included in CBI benefits, its adherence to international trade regulations, and equitable access of U.S. products to its market.

In principle, the CBI was based on three concepts: free trade, economic assistance, and investment. The goals were to generate foreign currency earnings, create new jobs, and increase production levels; these goals were to be met by establishing free access to the U.S. market for Caribbean products during twelve years, providing $350 million toward solving the balance of payments problem in some countries, and working toward the development of local infrastructures, while creating tax rebates for U.S. companies investing in the Caribbean Basin.[68]

The establishment of a unilateral duty-free zone in the Caribbean Basin led to duty-free access of certain Caribbean products into the United States. The articles on this list had to be grown, produced, or manufactured in one of the beneficiary countries and had to comply with certain rules of origin. For example, the product was required to be imported directly from the United States, at least 35 percent of its aggregate value was required to be added in one or several of the beneficiary countries, and those products containing foreign components would have to be transformed into substantially "new and different commercial articles." At the same time, however, a list of items was prepared that could be excluded from these requirements, among them textiles, footwear, and leather articles designed before the passing of the new law, and tuna, petroleum, and petroleum by-products. Special rules were set up to limit sugar imports, adhering to existing quotas established for certain countries and to the "competitive needs" criteria of the Generalized System of Preferences (GSP).[69]

The creation of a duty-free trade zone in the Caribbean Basin necessitated two other aspects of the CBI: in order to increase the Caribbean economies' export capacity, foreign investments had to be stimulated, and this, in turn, could only be achieved by improving the service infrastructure, which was to be developed on the basis of U.S. economic assistance.

All in all, twenty-one Caribbean Basin states were selected as beneficiary countries and six were excluded. Of the latter, three—Guyana, Nicaragua, and Suriname—were excluded on political grounds, and the other three (all small islands economically dependent on financing and tourism)—Anguilla, the Cayman Islands, and Turks and Caicos—were excluded because they failed to express their willingness to participate in the program.

The CBI announcement caused great expectations among the governments in the region, particularly in view of the "conservative tide" that was then sweeping the area. However, once the first promotional impact of the announcement began to wear away, its limited scope became evident. Since 87 percent of the Caribbean's total exports already enjoyed duty-free access to the U.S. market by virtue of the GSP program established in 1974 (which included 2,800 duty-free items), the creation of a duty-free zone had a limited effect on regional exports. The greatest advantages were offered to products such as rum, citrus fruits, and tobacco, all traditional export products, while highly important products such as sugar and textiles were subjected to protectionist measures tantamount to the establishment of quotas. Meanwhile, a report by the U.S. International Trade Commission (ITC) proposed that imports from CBI beneficiary countries should be reduced by 23.7 percent between 1983 and 1985.[70]

The recent decision of the United States to reduce sugar import quotas from the region by 41 percent has aggravated the situation and reaffirmed increasing U.S. protectionism, causing many of the measures provided for in the CBI to erode. This latest decision, for example, resulted in a reduction of exports from the principal CARICOM sugar producers from approximately 134,420 tons in 1984/85 and 95,000 tons in 1985/86 to 53,440 tons in 1986/87.[71]

Moreover, the CBI was irrelevant to the small islands and territories that lacked the adequate infrastructure to accommodate industrial investors; the bulk of economic assistance thus went to Central American countries and to the Dominican Republic, Haiti, and Jamaica. The CBI, furthermore, made no provisions for the crucial question of low and unstable prices of such products as sugar, bananas, and bauxite, which ranked among the principal causes of balance of payments problems in the non-Hispanic Caribbean.

In addition, tax rebates and fiscal incentives were aimed mainly at U.S. corporations establishing themselves in the Caribbean and were linked to the express interests of the Caribbean/Central American Action (C/CAA) group, which was created in 1980 with the financial support of multinational giants such as Alcoa, Gulf and Western, Chase Manhattan Bank, Intercontinental Hotels, Tesoro Petroleum, and United Brand.

Despite the fact that one of the main objectives of the CBI was to attract U.S. investment to the Caribbean, the prevailing tendency has not been encouraging. In the first place, investments have been aimed at sectors that were traditionally attractive to foreign investment—natural resources, tourism, and finance—while the inflow of funds to the manufacturing sector has been directed mainly to the garment industry and to electronic assembly plants, resulting in a limited "Taiwanization" of some economies. Second, U.S. investments, which had begun to decrease between 1978 and 1981, continued to do so in subsequent years. In general, there has been a tendency to decapitalize transnational enterprises. This tendency has not been reversed, not even by the efforts of some government agencies promoting the CBI and offering advice to U.S. investors in the Caribbean Basin. This tendency is clearly illustrated by the departure of Alcan and Gulf and Western from the Dominican Republic, Reynolds Metal from Jamaica, and Lago from Aruba, as well as by the sale of a Texaco refinery to the Trinidad and Tobago government.

In addition, increased external obligations of the governments in the region have led to economic contraction and the devaluation of local currencies, generating a climate of economic instability and uncertainty that is hardly conducive to foreign investments.

The distribution of the $350 million in assistance demonstrated that the CBI would not respond to the Caribbean countries' true needs, but to political interests. While a CARICOM report in 1982 called attention to the pressing need for $580 million in assistance for the Caribbean islands—a figure derived from the $4 billion annual deficit in the regional balance of payments[72]—of the $350 million approved, $128 million was allocated to El Salvador (a figure later reduced to $75 million). The other major beneficiaries were Costa Rica ($70 million), Honduras ($35 million), and Guatemala ($10 million) in Central America; and Jamaica ($50 million), Dominican Republic ($41 million), and Haiti ($10 million) in the island Caribbean states. The Eastern Caribbean states were allotted only $10 million to distribute among themselves. The assistance actually had a very limited impact on the island economies, since it was aimed most particularly at the private sector. Its most significant impact was in addressing the balance of payments problem, and, indeed, this has turned out to be the program's single effective element.

The CBI's most controversial element has been its bilateral nature. The White House unilaterally selected the CBI beneficiaries and negotiated the flow of economic assistance directly with the respective governments, bypassing regional organizations such as the Caribbean Development Bank and the Central American Bank for Economic Integration. The combination of a plan oriented to the private sector and the preference for bilateralism, disregarding regional organizations and multilateral negotiations, has been the main focus of criticism directed at the CBI by some governments in the region. However, in the United States, where responsibility for promoting the initiative lay with the government, strategic considerations found their way into market decisions.

In essence, an analysis of the short-term effects of the CBI shows that: (1) trade and tariff provisions have not been of particular benefit to the countries in the region, with the exception of certain governments that were granted special privileges by the United States; (2) economic assistance has in fact diminished without, however, having contributed toward solving the pressing needs of Caribbean societies or significantly stimulating local production; and (3) U.S. investments in the region, far from increasing, have tended to decrease in recent years. Indeed, very few Caribbean products have been favored by the new import regulations, and local conditions have not lent themselves to a substantial increase in foreign investment.

In contrast, Canada has developed an effective assistance policy in the Caribbean through its Caribcan program, though it is a less relevant geopolitical actor in the region, with no strategic interests. As a result, there is significant Canadian involvement, particularly in the Commonwealth Caribbean states.

Although at present, Canadian trade with the Caribbean shows signs of decreasing, the Caribbean remains one of the most profitable areas of Canadian foreign trade, to the extent that in 1981 Canada had a positive balance of trade with the region amounting to $368 million.[73]

Substantial Canadian investment has been made in the Caribbean, especially in financing, bauxite, and transportation. In the 1960s, almost half of Canadian investment in the Third World was in the Caribbean, and, at present, despite increasing investments in Latin America, one-fourth of Canadian investment in the Third World is still placed in the region.[74] Of the four largest banks in the Caribbean, three are Canadian: Royal Bank of Canada, the Bank of Nova Scotia, and the Imperial Canadian Bank of Commerce.[75]

Moreover, the Canadian agency for economic assistance to the region—the Canadian International Development Agency (CIDA)—offers extensive government aid, which in the long run has favored the expansion of these investments, based on the substantial support of Canadian private capital. A major portion of economic assistance, however, is channeled toward development of infrastructures in Caribbean Basin countries, frequently diverging from the lines of U.S. assistance. At present, Canada is providing assistance to the region, particularly to the English-speaking Caribbean, in the amount of

Can$ 35 million annually. Plans existed for 1987 to double the amount of this economic assistance, mainly through the Caribbean Development Bank, nongovernmental organizations, and an industrial cooperation agreement, as well as through existing bilateral agreements.[76]

Relations with Latin America

The emergence of new English-speaking states in the Caribbean and their inclusion in the international system was marked, from the start, by the rise of significant differences with the Latin American states, both at the political and the economic level. The fact that Latin America had joined the system much earlier and the development of the inter-American system, with its distinctive features, exacerbated these differences.

In the 1960s, for example, the English-speaking Caribbean states requested accession to the Organization of American States (OAS). As already noted, Jamaica and Trinidad and Tobago achieved independence in 1962, bringing to a halt any aspirations for political integration of the English-speaking Caribbean territories. Soon after they became independent, these states expressed the wish to join the OAS. The general reaction of the Latin American states was one of restraint and distrust, and the debate that ensued in regard to the legitimacy of this aspiration effectively delayed the entry of these English-speaking Caribbean states into the OAS for several years.[77] Latin American reluctance was due to two main perceptions: first, there was the feeling that these states had not entirely severed their colonial ties with Great Britain, a suspicion later confirmed when they joined the Commonwealth in 1965; and second, given the prevailing atmosphere in the organization at the time, the member states had misgivings about their establishing ties with Cuba. In 1972, Jamaica, Trinidad, Barbados, and Guyana all established diplomatic relations with Fidel Castro's revolutionary government. This did open the way for similar initiatives by some Latin American countries.

The Caribbean states, assuming a position similar to that of Canada, were distrustful of an organization that was perceived as an appendage of U.S. policy in the hemisphere. However, a decisive argument in favor of joining the OAS was that, at the time, membership was a prerequisite for receiving credit from the Inter-American Development Bank. This argument ultimately contributed to increasing participation in the organization by English-speaking states.[78]

Another factor affecting West Indian membership was Article 8 of the OAS Charter, which prevented any state that had a border conflict with a member state from joining the organization. This situation particularly affected Guyana, because of the Venezuelan claim to the Esequibo territory. Guyana resented the lack of regional consultation when Trinidad and Jamaica applied to join the OAS,[79] and it was not able to ask for IDB assistance until 1975, when the prerequisite of OAS membership was lifted.

The accession of Jamaica and Trinidad to the OAS did not relax mutual sensitivities between the Latin American states and the English-speaking Caribbean states. In practice, it led to a marked differentiation between both groups of nations and the creation of blocs, reinforced when other Caribbean states joined the organization as they gained independence. As mentioned elsewhere, the Caribbean representatives voiced numerous complaints about the OAS as an "Iberian-American" organization that generally did not take sufficiently into account the interests of the English-speaking Caribbean states.[80]

Similar differences arose within the United Nations, where separate blocs also began to form. Initial agreement had been reached between both groups in regard to supporting the decolonization processes, denouncing colonialism and racism, and achieving the rapid incorporation of the English-speaking states into the Latin American Group (GRULA). Nevertheless, political disagreement frequently erupted within the GRULA,[81] though some coordination was achieved in regard to economic topics. In addition to these differences, efforts by each group to place their respective representatives as coordinators of the various UN commissions and agencies have created a rivalry that continues to this day, in the context of the international body.[82]

In other international organizations, such as the Movement of Non-Aligned Countries, where the Latin American participation has traditionally been more limited than that of the English-speaking Caribbean states, political differences also mark the relationship between both groups. Moreover, alignment frequently reflects existing territorial conflicts.[83] The ties of the English-speaking Caribbean states to the Commonwealth have also contributed to the Latin American perception that these states are prone to act in accordance with British interests.[84]

Tensions between the Latin American and the Caribbean states reached a climax in the OAS in 1982 as a result of positions taken in regard to the South Atlantic conflict. With the exception of Grenada, then under the revolutionary government of the New Jewel Movement, the English-speaking Caribbean states supported Great Britain and aligned themselves against the Argentine intervention in the Malvinas/Falklands.[85]

Thus, in general terms, ethnohistorical, political, and territorial differences have been a considerable obstacle to attempts at political coordination between both groups of nations within international forums. In the area of economic cooperation, these differences have likewise prevailed, despite some agreement during the 1970s in respect to South-South cooperation and to the creation of a New International Economic Order.

The creation of regional and subregional integration schemes occurred several years earlier in Latin America than in the Caribbean, and Caribbean states were generally excluded from them.[86] Among the principal obstacles to Caribbean participation were the diverse size, population, economic potential, and degree of development of these states, to say nothing of their differences from the Latin American states. Diversity presented an obstacle for those who conceived the region in relatively homogeneous economic terms.

Although, from an ethnohistorical point of view, a definition of the Caribbean that encompassed the island Caribbean, Belize, and the Guianas might suggest a unitary perspective of the region, the differences existing between Cuba, Haiti, and St. Lucia, for example—all located within one regional context—are particularly striking. If the concept is extended to include continental Latin American countries, then the situation becomes even more complex, since countries with greater economic development would have to be taken into account—e.g., Mexico, Venezuela, and Colombia (all identifying with a "Caribbean orientation") and the countries of Central America, a subregion known for its common economic and social problems where, however, substantial differences can also be observed.[87]

As a result of the internal diversity of the Latin American states and their differences with the Caribbean countries, the possibilities for Caribbean participation in regional schemes, ranging from the Latin American Free Trade Association (LAFTA), the broadest regional integration scheme to date, to subsequent subregional initiatives such as the Central American Common Market (CACM) and the Andean Pact, have traditionally been quite limited. The creation of CARIFTA in 1967 and CARICOM in 1973, with the participation of the English-speaking Caribbean states and excluding other island states, did not contribute to overcoming the barriers between Latin America and the English-speaking Caribbean.

Consequently, economic integration initiatives have never been implemented by the English-speaking Caribbean and the Latin American states. Multilateral economic cooperation efforts have been almost entirely limited to the establishment of ECLAC and SELA, which are specific mechanisms of limited scope.

The Economic Commission for Latin America and the Caribbean (ECLAC) created a subregional office in Port of Spain in 1965; it also founded the Caribbean Development and Cooperation Committee (CDCC) in 1975 as a "permanent intergovernmental subsidiary organization of ECLAC." The CDCC has eighteen members: twelve members of CARICOM (of which seven belong to the Organization of Eastern Caribbean States), plus Cuba, Bahamas, Dominican Republic, Haiti, the Netherlands Antilles, and Suriname. Its objectives are to promote the social and economic development of its individual members, to promote economic coordination in the Caribbean, and to facilitate economic cooperation between its members and other ECLAC members, as well as with Latin American economic integration groupings such as the Latin American Integration Association (ALADI), the CACM, the Andean

Group, and other subregional organizations. This last objective, however, has not been realized.

CDCC activities overlap with those of ECLAC's subregional office in Port of Spain, and it has not acquired a status similar to it or to that of other ECLAC subregional offices. It has not attained influence comparable to that of the Latin American states. This situation has led to protests by the Caribbean countries and tensions with the Latin American states. Some analysts have pointed out that while the activities of ECLAC and its offices tend to reflect UN dynamics, the CDCC reflects more closely the expectations of the Caribbean states.[88]

The creation of the Latin American Economic System (SELA) in the same year as the CDCC seemingly opened up new possibilities for coordinated economic action by Latin America and the Caribbean. The common ideology of its principal promoters—President Echeverría of Mexico, President Carlos Andrés Pérez of Venezuela, and Prime Minister Michael Manley of Jamaica—who already agreed on the need to create a New International Economic Order and shared an intention to further South-South relations, was apparently to initiate a period of closer cooperation between Latin America and the Caribbean. The exclusion of the United States and the inclusion of Cuba in the new organization and its differentiation from the OAS and the UN, gave it an express regional and "Third World" bias. Its fundamental objectives focused on the promotion of regional cooperation and on the establishment of a permanent system for consultation and coordination among the member states, with a view to adopting similar economic and social policies and strategies.

Nevertheless, the ideological concepts that inspired the founders were not necessarily shared by the remaining English-speaking Caribbean states that joined SELA—Barbados, Trinidad and Tobago, Grenada, and, to a lesser extent, Guyana. Grenada modified its stance, however, after the rise of the New Jewel Movement in 1979. "It can be said that the Consultation and Coordination area was of interest to the Caribbean states, exclusively for Jamaica, and since the Bishop government, also for Grenada."[89] A drastic change took place in the position of both islands after the political transformations experienced in the 1980s.

The Caribbean states have tended toward limited participation both in the organization as a whole and in its action committees and permanent commissions. A quick review shows that Barbados participates in none, Guyana in one, Trinidad and Tobago and Grenada in two, while Jamaica has been included in four. More recently, Grenada has repeatedly expressed its desire to withdraw[90] and has remained a member only due to Venezuelan pressure.

Efforts to design a specific cooperation program between the non-Hispanic Caribbean countries and the Latin American states, despite the special recommendations of the Third Biennial Programme of 1986, have been fruitless, mainly owing to the lack of response by the respective governments of both groups of nations.[91] Multilateral cooperation experiments, such as the Caribbean Multinational Shipping Company (NAMUCAR) to deal with shipping problems, and efforts at coordination among commodity producers and exporters, such as the Latin American and Caribbean Group of Sugar Exporting Countries (GEPLACEA)—launched in the 1970s and involving both groups of states—have not met with success, and have produced, instead, new sources of tension among participants.

A notable exception in this series of difficulties in establishing multilateral forms of cooperation has been the participation of Venezuela, Mexico, and Colombia in the Caribbean Development Bank. The importance of the San José Agreement, signed by Venezuela and Mexico to provide oil to the Caribbean Basin states, is also noteworthy.

However, cooperation initiatives between both groups seem to be working more smoothly at the bilateral level, especially in relation to the "Caribbean" policies designed by the so-called Latin American "middle powers" involved in the region.

Aside from Cuba, which, as shall be pointed out later, sustained a specific policy toward the region throughout the 1970s—reinforced by its dual identification as an Afro-Latin American and Caribbean country and by its "Third World" projection—the other Latin American countries that have developed an active Caribbean policy are Mexico, Venezuela, Colombia, and more recently, Brazil.

During the 1970s, within the framework of the Third World policy promoted by President Echeverría, Mexico formulated a specific policy vis-à-vis the Caribbean, occasionally coordinating with President Carlos Andrés Pérez of Venezuela. Though Mexico's involvement in the Caribbean is more recent than Venezuela's, it reacted to the times, aiming its regional action, especially at the Western Caribbean.Vaughn Lewis, describing this policy as "reactive or protective," argues that its limited deployment was due to Mexico's restricted identification with the region and that the policy was basically conditioned by policy toward Cuba and by Mexico's thorny relations with the United States.[92] In fact, the impulse that led to the initiative diminished in later administrations, as the country's economic crisis deepened, so that many of the early assistance and cooperation programs for Caribbean states were progressively eliminated.[93]

In 1980 Mexico and Venezuela established a petroleum facility for the Caribbean through the San José Agreement, which provided for an annual contribution of $300 million in oil products, and established a set of measures which lifted or substantially reduced duties on various imports from the Caribbean and Central American countries. In the island Caribbean, this scheme was first applied to Barbados, Jamaica, and the Dominican Republic, and later to other countries. The program provided oil for the internal consumption of the beneficiary countries, together with credit for 30 percent of outstanding debts.

Mexico set in motion, at both the multilateral and bilateral levels, other Caribbean initiatives as well, mostly in relation to trade treaties. In July 1974 an intergovernmental committee was formed in conjunction with the CARICOM countries. The committee began implementing its goals in 1980, with the participation of the Mexican Foreign Trade Institute and the Mexican Private Enterprise Council for International Affairs (CEMAI). Trade treaties were entered into with the Bahamas, Jamaica, Guyana, and Trinidad and Tobago, and a series of programs was implemented with Cuba and the Dominican Republic.[94] However, Mexican interest in the Caribbean later diminished as a result of a shift to the Pacific in its foreign policy priorities.

Venezuela, which outlined its own specific policy toward the region in the late 1960s, subsequently ascribed increasing importance to its Caribbean policy. Taking advantage of the favorable conditions resulting from the increase in oil prices during the 1973–1974 world oil crisis, the Carlos Andrés Pérez government furthered this tendency.[95] The Venezuelan Investment Fund (FIV) played a leading role by directing the bulk of economic assistance to the region, in the framework of PROCA. The FIV administered a special Caribbean fund derived from deposits made in the central banks of the beneficiary countries for financing development programs and energy cooperation projects; these funds could also be used to purchase Venezuelan goods or to finance preinvestment projects.[96] It should be pointed out, moreover, that in terms of multilateral agreements, Venezuela was one of the first Latin American countries to become an active member of the Caribbean Development Bank (CDB), in 1975.

Venezuela has also, however, entered frequently into bilateral agreements. In addition to its fishing agreements with Trinidad and Tobago and with Suriname, it has also implemented agreements for bauxite production with the latter, as well as with Jamaica and, more recently, Guyana. It has developed economic, scientific, and technical cooperation programs with Suriname and Eastern Caribbean states. The Venezuelan private sector has been active in the region since the 1970s, with the establishment of a paper plant in St. Lucia and exports of cement, construction materials, textiles, and petrochemical supplies. Some of these initiatives have been channeled through the Foreign Trade Institute (ICE) and the Venezuelan Exporters' Association (AVEX). The abrupt fall in bolívar parity with the U.S. dollar, after the onset of the country's economic crisis,[97] has also reinforced this process.

During the Lusinchi administration, policy toward the region was more closely defined, focusing on cooperation programs developed with an emphasis on "shared responsibility," and on the implementation of a more active cultural policy, aimed at making Venezuela better known among the non-Hispanic Caribbean states.[98]

Colombia set out an economic cooperation policy toward the Caribbean in the 1970s, aimed particularly at the Netherlands Antilles, whereby lines of credit were opened up for Colombian imports. In the early 1980s Colombia expanded this policy to the Eastern Caribbean states, signing agreements with Barbados and Jamaica and setting up a scheme to compensate for transportation costs to Guyana, Suriname, and the Netherlands Antilles. In addition to these initiatives, Colombia also participates in the CDB; and, in 1981, in the context of the Amazon treaty, it signed an extensive economic cooperation agreement with Guyana.[99] However, as in Mexico, Colombian interest in the Caribbean progressively diminished in favor of a new emphasis on the Pacific.

Since the late 1970s, a new continental actor, Brazil, has made its appearance in the region, especially following the signing of the Amazon treaty. During the 1980s, Brazil increased its bilateral cooperation agreements with Caribbean countries, starting with the creation of joint commissions with Guyana, Suriname, and Trinidad and Tobago. Its contribution to the Caribbean Development Fund, made through the IDB, should be seen as part of its increasing involvement in the Caribbean, particularly with these three countries, and with certain private initiatives in the Eastern Caribbean tourist industry. Brazil also implemented cooperative agreements with Guyana and Suriname in the areas of science and technology, providing assistance to the former for expanding the roadways infrastructure and to the latter for improving telephone communications. In 1983 Brazil signed military assistance agreements with both of these countries.[100] Furthermore, agreements have been made between the Brazilian and Trinidadian national oil companies.

The Caribbean policies of the Latin American regional powers are frequently influenced by regional strategic and geopolitical considerations outside the scope of the East-West conflict. In this regard, it is important to bear in mind existing rivalries between them in relation to persisting geopolitical doctrines—this is particularly true of Brazil and Colombia. In fact, considerations of this sort are often found to influence policymaking in terms of strategically important zones, inasmuch as Latin American interests in the region have more to do with security and national influence than with economic factors.

The non-Hispanic Caribbean countries likewise place security and political stability in the zone high on their foreign policy agenda, particularly since the Grenada crisis. Historically, such considerations had been relegated to second place, owing to the importance attached to economic relations and to stimulating local economic development. In this context, Latin America had been of secondary interest to these countries, which looked instead to the former colonial European metropolitan centers and to the United States and Canada as potential sources of economic assistance, and toward the African states, linked ethnohistorically to their populations, for cultural ties.

Certain "Latin American doctrines" are, however, to be found in the English-speaking Caribbean. These range from the policy outlined by Eric

Williams, which questioned Latin American involvement in the region, especially Venezuela's presence, to that put forward by Michael Manley, which stressed the common "Third World" interests of Latin American and Caribbean countries.

Aside from these specific "doctrines," a significant shift has nevertheless been observed in recent years in the attitude of some of the non-Hispanic governments, which are beginning to regard relations with Latin America as a "third path," an alternative to the choices governed by superpower confrontation. This change in attitude, from indifference and suspicion to pragmatism in relations with Latin America, is as yet barely discernible and can be seen most clearly in the increase in trade between the two regions.[101]

Notes

1. Leslie Manigat: "Geopolítica de las relaciones de Venezuela con el Caribe," in *Geopolítica de las relaciones de Venezuela con el Caribe,* edited by Andres Serbin, Caracas: Fondo Editorial Acta Científica, 1983, p. 34.
2. See Anthony Maingot: "Las percepciones como realidades: EEUU, Venezuela y Cuba en el Caribe," in *Entre la autonomía y la subordinación. Política exterior de los países latinoamericanos,* edited by Heraldo Muñoz and Joseph Tulchin, Buenos Aires: Grupo Editor Latinoamericano, 1984. The English version of the book has been published under the title *Latin American Nations in World Politics,* Boulder, Colo.: Westview Press, 1984.
3. Grupo de Trabajo del Consejo Atlántico sobre la Cuenca del Caribe: "Intereses occidentales y opciones políticas de los EEUU en la Cuenca del Caribe: documento sobre política," in *Intereses occidentales y política de Estados Unidos en el Caribe,* edited by James R. Greene and Brent Scowcroft, Buenos Aires: Grupo Editor Latinoamericano, 1985, p. 29. The English version of the book has been published as *Western Interests and U.S. Policy Option in the Caribbean Basin,* Boston: Delgeschlager, Gunn and Haim, 1984.
4. Idem.
5. Isabel Jaramillo: "Problemas de seguridad interamericana," manuscript, s/f, p. 23.
6. Jack Child: "Variables para la política estadounidense en la Cuenca del Caribe en la década de 1980: Seguridad," in *Intereses occidentales y política de Estados Unidos en el Caribe,* edited by James Greene and Brent Scowcroft, Buenos Aires: Grupo Editor Latinoamericano, 1985, pp. 151–156.
7. See Demetrio Boersner: "Una estrategia tercermundista para el Caribe," in *Nueva Sociedad,* 77 (1978) and Gonzalo Martner: "La Cuenca del Caribe: futuro centro de desarrollo latinoamericano," in *Nueva Sociedad,* 24 (1976).
8. See Andres Serbin: *Etnocentrismo y geopolítica. Las relaciones entre América Latina y el Caribe de habla inglesa,* Caracas: Academia Nacional de la Historia, 1990.
9. See Andres Serbin: "Las relaciones entre América Latina y el Caribe: obstáculos y dificultades," in *A la espera de una nueva etapa. Anuario de políticas exteriores latinoamericanas,* edited by Heraldo Muñoz, Caracas: Nueva Sociedad/Prospel, 1989.
10. Luis Maira: *Los intereses políticos y estratégicos de Estados Unidos en América del Sur*, working paper, Santiago: Comisión Sudamericana de Paz, 1989, pp. 33–40.

11. See Ray S. Cline: *World Power Trends and U.S. Foreign Policy for the 1980s,* Boulder, Colo.: Westview Press, 1980.

12. Isabel Jaramillo: "Medio Oriente y 'Cuenca del Caribe': fuerza de paz o de intervención?" in *Cuadernos de Nuestra América,* Vol. 1, 1 (1984), p. 84.

13. Luis Maira: "Caribbean State Systems and Middle-Status Powers: The Cases of Mexico, Venezuela and Cuba," in *The New Caribbean: Decolonization, Democracy and Development,* edited by Carl Stone and Paget Henry, Philadelphia: Inter-American Political Series, ISHI, 1983, pp. 184–185.

14. See Guillermo Morón: *Historia de América Latina,* Caracas: Equinoccio, 1978.

15. See David Lowenthal: *West Indian Societies,* New York: Oxford University Press, 1972, and Barry Levine: "Geopolitical and Cultural Competition in the Caribbean," in *The New Cuban Presence in the Caribbean,* edited by Barry Levine, Boulder, Colo.: Westview Press, 1983.

16. See The Resource Center: *Focus on the Eastern Caribbean: Bananas, Bucks and Boots,* Albuquerque, 1984.

17. See Anthony Peter González: "Relaciones económicas de Estados Unidos con el Caribe," in *Capítulos del Sela,* 7 (1984).

18. See ibid., and Barry, T., B. Wood, and D. Preusch: *The Other Side of Paradise: Foreign Control in the Caribbean,* New York: Grove Press, 1984.

19. See Table 1.1.

20. Exceptions to the Westminster parliamentary model can be found in the Cooperative Republic of Guyana and in Trinidad and Tobago, which became a republic in the late 1980s. The Grenadan revolutionary process is a paradoxical case in which the governor appointed by the Crown "coexisted" with the GRP and ultimately invited the U.S. invasion.

21. See Rita Giacalone: "Antillas Neerlandesas: en búsqueda de un nuevo perfil," in *Nueva Sociedad,* 91 (1987) and Iraima Quiroz de Mommer: "La política petrolera venezolana frente a la refinería de Curazao," in *Venezuela y las relaciones internacionales en la Cuenca del Caribe,* edited by Andres Serbin, Caracas: ILDIS/AVECA, 1987.

22. See Roland Ely: "Guyana y Surinam frente al Coloso del Sur", in Ibid.; and Andres Serbin: "Surinam en el marco regional e internacional," in *Las políticas exteriores de América Latina y el Caribe: un balance de esperanzas,* edited by Heraldo Muñoz, Buenos Aires: Grupo Editor Latinoamericano, 1988.

23. See Ibid,; and Barry et al., *The Other Side of Paradise.*

24. See Barry et al., *The Other Side of Paradise.*

25. Ibid., p. 148.

26. Ibid., p. 246.

27. Anthony Bryan: "The CARICOM and Latin American Integration Experiences: Observations on Theoretical Origins and Comparative Performance," in *CARICOM Bulletin,* 4 (1983), p. 3.

28. See Angel Quintero Rivera: "The Socio-Political Background to the Emergence of the Puerto Rican Model as a Strategy of Development," in *Contemporary Caribbean: A Sociological Reader,* edited by Susan Craig, Maracas: The College Press, 1982.

29. Clive Thomas: "From Colony to State Capitalism (Alternative Paths of Development in the Caribbean)," in *Transition,* 5 (1982), pp. 7–8.

30. Jay Mandle: *Patterns of Caribbean Development,* New York: Gordon and Breach, 1982, p. 57.

31. Bryan: "CARICOM and Latin American Integration," p. 6.

32. Jay Mandle: "Ideologies of Development," in *Transition,* 2, 1 (1979), pp. 40–47.

33. See Andres Serbin: *Etnicidad, clase y nación en la cultura política del Caribe de habla inglesa,* Caracas: Academia Nacional de la Historia, 1987.

34. Thomas: "From Colony to State Capitalism," p. 11.

35. Armando López Coll: *La colaboración y la integración económicas en el Caribe,* Havana: Editorial de Ciencias Sociales, 1983, p. 56.

36. Mandle: *Patterns of Caribbean Development,* p. 60.

37. López Coll: *La colaboración y la integración,* p.53.

38. A similar process occurred in Suriname, with Alcan and Billiton in bauxite production.

39. López Coll: *La colaboración y la integración,* p. 53.

40. Franklin W. Knight: *The Caribbean: The Genesis of a Fragmented Nationalism,* New York: Oxford University Press, 1978, p. 208.

41. The list of U.S. firms operating in the English-speaking Caribbean includes over eight hundred companies, as opposed to eighty-five British companies. A similar situation exists in Jamaica, where the proportion is ten to one, respectively. See The Resource Center: *Focus on the Eastern Caribbean.*

42. See Andres Serbin: *Etnicidad,* and "Socialismo y nacionalismo en la ideología del Caribe de habla inglesa," in *Revista Occidental,* 1, 4 (1982).

43. Mandle: "Ideologies of Development," p. 45.

44. See Andres Serbin: "Surinam en el marco regional e internacional," in *Las políticas exteriores de América Latina y el Caribe: un balance de esperanzas,* edited by Heraldo Muñoz, Buenos Aires: Grupo Editor Latinoamericano/Prospel, 1988.

45. For a more detailed analysis, see Anthony Bryan: "The CARICOM and Latin American Integration Experiences: Observations on Theoretical Origins and Comparative Performance," in *CARICOM Bulletin,* 4 (1983), and Andres Serbin: *Etnicidad,* in regard to the New World Group. Also, Glenn Sankatsing: *Caribbean Social Sciences: An Assessment,* Caracas: UNESCO, 1988.

46. R. Greenwood and S. Hamber: *Development and Decolonization,* London: Macmillan Caribbean, 1980, p. 186, and Isaac Dookhan: *A Post Emancipation History of the West Indies,* London: Collins, 1982, p. 46.

47. Ibid., p. 86.

48. Ibid., p. 87.

49. Hermmanus Hoetink: "The Windward Islands of the Netherlands Antilles: Some Recent Developments," paper submitted to the International Colloquium on Eastern Caribbean Geopolitics, Oxford University, January 1988, p. 3.

50. See Christian Girault: "Les Caraibes de l'Est: Geographie politique d'un archipiel éclaté," and Fred Constant: "Décentralisation et politique aux Antilles Françaises (1981–1987)," papers submitted to the International Colloquium on Eastern Caribbean Geopolitics, Oxford University, January 1988. The Communist party of Guadeloupe recently adopted a pro-independence stance, openly breaking with its positions to date and with existing agreements with the socialists. See *Caribbean Insight,* April 1988.

51. See Barry et al.: *The Other Side of Paradise.* A more recent and detailed analysis is found in David Lewis: "República asociada y/en libertad? El futuro de Puerto Rico." in *Nueva Sociedad,* 93 (1988).

52. Bryan: "Commonwealth Caribbean," p. 4.

53. Ibid., p.8; and Anthony Payne: "Wither CARICOM? The Performance and Prospects of Caribbean Integration in the 1980s," in *International Journal,* 40 (1985), p. 224.

54. Bryan: "Commonwealth Caribbean," p. 10.

55. Payne: "Whither CARICOM," p. 226.

56. Bryan: "Commonwealth Caribbean," p. 11.

57. *Caribbean Contact,* August 1987.

58. Idem.

59. *Caribbean Contact,* July and August 1987.

60. Idem.

61. CEPAL: "Cooperación entre el Caribe y América Latina," E/CEPAL/SES 20/G. 29 (March 1984), p. 18.

62. Ibid., p. 28.

63. See Paul Sutton: "The Sugar Protocol of the Lomé Conventions and the Caribbean," in *Dual Legacies in the Contemporary Caribbean: Continuing Aspects of British and French Dominion,* edited by Paul Sutton, London: Frank Cass, 1986. A more detailed discussion on relations between the OECS and the European Community may be found in Paul Sutton: "EEC Development Assistance in the Eastern Caribbean," paper submitted to the International Colloquium on Eastern Caribbean Geopolitics, Oxford University, January 1988.

64. See Barry et al., *The Other Side of Paradise.*

65. See Guillermo Hillcoat and Carlos Quenan: "La Iniciativa de la Cuenca del Caribe: antecedentes y perspectivas," in *Venezuela y las relaciones internacionales en la Cuenca del Caribe,* edited by Andres Serbin, Caracas: ILDIS/AVECA, 1987, and Anthony Peter González: "Relaciones Económicas de Estados Unidos con el Caribe," in *Capítulos del SELA,* 7 (1984).

66. Ibid.

67. See United States Information Service: *La Iniciativa de la Cuenca del Caribe,* Washington, D.C.: USIS, 1985.

68. See Guillermo Hillcoat and Carlos Quenan: *La Iniciativa.*

69. González: "Relaciones económicas," p. 29.

70. Idem.

71. Reuters wire, in *El Nacional,* Caracas, 23 August 1986.

72. Gonzàlez: "Relaciones económicas," p. 33.

73. Barry et al., *The Other Side of Paradise,"* pp. 221–222.

74. Kari Levitt: "Canada and the Caribbean: An Assessment," in *The Caribbean and World Politics,* edited by Jorge Heine and Leslie Manigat, New York: Holmes and Meier, 1988, pp. 233–234.

75. Barry et al., *The Other Side of Paradise,* p. 222.

76. Levitt: "Canada and the Caribbean," pp. 235–237.

77. See Carlos Martínez Sotomayor: *El nuevo Caribe: La independencia de las colonias británicas,* Santiago: Andrés Bello, 1974.

78. Andres Serbin: "Procesos etnoculturales y percepciones mutuas en el desarrollo de las relaciones entre el Caribe de habla inglesa y América Latina," in *Bolétin de Estudios Latinoamericanos y del Caribe,* 38 (1985), pp. 92–93.

79. See Basil Ince: "Decision Making and Foreign Policy: Trinidad and Tobago Decision to Enter the OAS," in *Issues in Caribbean International Relations,* edited by Basil Ince, Anthony Bryan, Herb Addo, and Ramesh Ramsaran, Lanham: University Press of America, 1983.

80. See Serbin: *Etnocentrismo.*

81. See D. O. Mills and Vaughn A. Lewis: *Caribbean/Latin American Relations,* ECLAC/Caribbean Community Secretariat, October 1982.

82. The election of Mohamed Shahabudeen of Guyana to the International Court of Justice in The Hague, competing with a Brazilian candidate proposed by some Latin Americans, is an obvious illustration, within another international organization. See *Caribbean Times,* 27 November 1987, p. 12. More recently, competition for the chairmanship of the UN General Assembly in 1988 between Argentine Foreign Minister Dante Caputo and Nita Barrow of Barbados demonstrates the

differences between both groups of nations. In this case, pressure from Great Britain played a key role. See *Orbita Bip,* Caracas, April 1988, p. 15.

83. Nonalignment proclaimed by the English-speaking Caribbean states as a distinct feature of their foreign policy has led these states to actively participate in the Non-Aligned Movement. Venezuela's entry into the movement has thus been hindered because of its border dispute with Guyana, an active participant of the NAM.

84. See Payne: "Whither CARICOM."

85. See Roland Ely: *Olas de las Malvinas: Repercusiones del conflicto anglo-argentino en la Cuenca del Caribe,* Mérida, Venezuela: Libros Azul, 1983.

86. Not only English-speaking Caribbean states were excluded, but also Cuba, the Dominican Republic, and Haiti.

87. See William Demas' definition given in the Introduction to *The Restless Caribbean: Changing Patterns of International Relations,* edited by Richard Millet and Marvin Will, New York: Praeger, 1979. For a more detailed view of economic relations between Latin America and the Caribbean in the 1970s, see Héctor Hurtado: "Venezuela and the Caribbean: Integration of Integration," in *Studies on the Economic Integration of the Caribbean and Latin America,* Bogotá: Association of Caribbean Universities and Research Institutes, 1974.

88. See Mills and Lewis: *Caribbean/Latin American Relations.*

89. Héctor Torres: "El Caribe anglófono en el SELA"; ms, 1988, p. 14.

90. Ibid., p. 17.

91. Ibid., p. 18.

92. Vaughn A. Lewis: "Commonwealth Caribbean Relations with Hemispheric Middle Powers," in *Dependency Under Challenge: The Political Economy of the Commonwealth Caribbean,* edited by Anthony Payne and Paul Sutton, Manchester: University of Manchester Press, 1983, pp. 246–247.

93. See Bryan: "Commonwealth Caribbean"; Gill, "Cuba and Mexico"; and Maira, "Caribbean State Systems."

94. Mills and Lewis: *Caribbean/Latin American Relations,* p. 29.

95. Robert D. Bond: "Venezuela, la Cuenca del Caribe y la crisis en Centroamérica," in *Centroamérica: Crisis y Política Internacional,* Mexico City: Siglo XXI, 1982.

96. Victoria Casanovas: "Venezuela hacia el Caribe y la cooperación Sur-Sur," in *Venezuela y las relaciones internacionales en la Cuenca del Caribe,* edited by Andres Serbin, Caracas: ILDIS/AVECA, 1987, pp. 219, 225.

97. See Casanovas: "Venezuela hacia el Caribe," pp. 219, 225.

98. Interview with Venezuelan Special Ambassador for Caribbean Affairs François Moanack, Caracas, 5 May 1987.

99. Mills and Lewis: *Caribbean/Latin American Relations,* p. 30.

100. See Roland Ely: "Guyana y Suriname" and George Danns: "The Role of the Military in the National Security of Guyana," in *Militarization in the Non-Hispanic Caribbean,* edited by Alma Young and Dion Phillips, Boulder, Colo.: Lynne Rienner, 1986. For further details on Guyanese militarization, see George Danns: *Domination and Power in Guyana,* New Brunswick, N.J.: Transaction Books, 1982.

101. See Henry Gill and Juan de Castro: "Algunos aspectos de las relaciones comerciales entre el Caribe y América Latina," *Capítulos del SELA,* 7 (1984).

2
The Geopolitical Scene: Regional and Extraregional Actors

The CARICOM States

The general description of the English-speaking Caribbean states provided in the preceding chapter depicts them as prominent actors in the region. Moreover, coordination of the CARICOM member states' foreign policy has been, despite its ups and downs, a significant element in the geopolitical dynamics of the Caribbean.

During the 1970s, most of the English-speaking Caribbean states proclaimed their nonaligned stance, a position that was institutionally reinforced by their active participation in the Movement of Non-Aligned Countries. However, in the early 1980s the Caribbean states' foreign policy underwent considerable change, causing this image to wane. The fact that the "socialist" experiences of Jamaica, Guyana, and Grenada have been drastically reversed can be pointed to as a first landmark in this process.

In Jamaica, the victory of the Jamaica Labour Party (JLP) in 1980 and the rise to power of the Edward Seaga government, following destabilizing pressures exerted by the IMF and by the United States on the Michael Manley government, led to alignment with U.S. interests in the region. Jamaica soon became the showcase for the "magic of the market" solution advocated by the United States for the Caribbean. Indeed, the Reagan administration tried to convert this Caribbean state into a model of capitalist development for the Third World, in contrast with Manley's thwarted attempts at a "noncapitalist development path," which had precipitated the U.S. pressures and the stampede of departing foreign investments during the second half of the 1970s.

Soon after the JLP's electoral victory, the IMF, which throughout the preceding years had reacted vigorously against Manley's economic policies, offered $650 million to Jamaica under particularly flexible terms.[1] Bilateral aid from the United States rose abruptly from $14 million during the last year of the Manley government to over $200 million in the first two years of the Seaga government.[2] At the same time, the Reagan administration purchased bauxite, provided advisory services to the Seaga government on how to attract foreign investments (through a committee organized by David Rockefeller), and injected economic assistance into the country through the Agency for International Development (USAID).[3]

As a result, Jamaica became the unconditional ally of the United States in the region, drastically breaking off relations and discontinuing assistance and cooperation programs with Cuba. Jamaica's participation and support of the United States in the Grenada invasion of October 1983, followed by early elections that once again favored Seaga, should be seen in this light. Seaga's new electoral victory, however, occurred in the context of a boycott by Manley's People's National Party, thus allowing Seaga to govern with no parliamentary opposition.

Meanwhile, in 1982, the fall in the price of bauxite, as a result of the world recession, and an increase in external indebtedness began to adversely affect the island's economy. The Jamaican dollar was subsequently dramatically devalued by 43 percent. In the following years the country's economic situation continued to deteriorate, with Jamaica sustaining the largest external debt in CARICOM, nearing the $3 billion figure. This situation, together with increased public support of Manley in the late 1980s and a significant shift in Manley's attitude toward the United States, has not, however, hindered Seaga's consistent policy of fully identifying with U.S. interests.[4] During the Reagan administration, military aid and training for Jamaica increased considerably to $4 million in 1984, while Jamaican training agreements were entered into with the Puerto Rican National Guard as of 1982.[5]

In Guyana, the nonaligned position that led the government of Forbes Burnham to establish ties not only with Cuba, but with the USSR, Eastern European countries, and China as well, eventually shifted during the early 1980s, owing, on the one hand, to the lack of a consistent response to requests for economic assistance from the socialist bloc, and on the other hand, to U.S. pressure. Despite rapprochement between Guyana and Cuba during the 1970s, the latter was never actually able to perceive Guyana as a reliable ally, in part because of persecution by the Burnham government and by his party, the People's National Congress, against the Marxist-Leninist People's Progressive Party led by Cheddi Jagan. Extensive corruption and racial tensions, which Burnham himself fueled, and the assassination in June 1980 of Walter Rodney, leader of the Working People Alliance, also contributed to a cooling of Cuban-Guyanese relations.

In the meantime, the United States never ceased to exert pressure on the Guyana government, which had been identified with the establishment of "cooperative socialism" since 1973. The United States went so far as to veto a loan of $20 million from the Inter-American Development Bank in 1980 and to jeopardize Guyanese relations with the IMF.[6] As the economic crisis intensified and the assistance expected from Cuba and the socialist bloc did not materialize in the volumes desired by the Burnham government, relations with the United States began to shift.

The incorporation of Guyana as a CBI beneficiary country contributed to bringing this Caribbean state back into the U.S. sphere of influence. During Burnham's last years and especially after the rise to power of President Hoyte, who succeeded him through elections plagued with accusations of fraud, the situation was definitely reversed, and Guyana has since then progressively abandoned its ties with the socialist bloc. Guyana's rapprochement and improved relations with Venezuela in the late 1980s follows this reversal.

The economic reasons for the change in Guyanese foreign policy were compounded by strategic reasons. Although a substantial amount of military assistance to Guyana came from Cuba and North Korea in the late 1970s, another significant source of aid in this field was Brazil, whose geopolitical proximity raised the question of the risks involved in Guyanese foreign policy. At the same time, beginning in 1981, the first efforts to establish military agreements with the United States, through the Military Education Training Program (IMET), quickly progressed so that by 1985, there were fifty Guyanese students participating in the program, and over $98,000 in military aid had been received from the United States.[7]

Grenada is another case in point, a landmark in the region's geopolitical scene. The overthrow of Prime Minister Eric Gairy in 1979 led to the rise to power of the New Jewel Movement, formed by a group of radical nationalists who were originally influenced by the Black Power movement. U.S. pressures dating from the period of the revolutionary government of Maurice Bishop only served to push the island further toward radicalization of its foreign policy. As a result, Grenada strengthened its ties with Cuba and the socialist bloc and was among those countries that formally supported the Soviet invasion of Afghanistan within the United Nations. However, during this same period, links with the EEC were also strengthened, as well as with Arab states and Latin American countries. Significantly, the Grenadan economy was the only Caribbean economy to show sustained growth during 1981/82.[8]

Grenada's diversification of international links did not keep the United States from perceiving the island nation as a threat to its interests in the region, even though the revolutionary government's economic program was not as radical as its foreign policy.[9] The Reagan administration was above all concerned that the construction of an airport at Point Salines, planned in order to accommodate greater tourist contingents, might become a possible Cuban base in the region.

Thus, when an internal conflict within the New Jewel Movement—between a radical Marxist sector led by Minister of the Economy Bernard Coard and the supporters of Maurice Bishop—led to Bishop's assassination, the event provided sufficient justification for the United States to intervene in Grenada. This intervention was carried out with the support of Jamaica, Barbados, and the Eastern Caribbean states, and under the pretext of protecting the lives of U.S. students living in Grenada and preventing generalized political instability in the region.[10]

In the elections that followed the intervention, and which took place in the presence of U.S. and Caribbean troops, U.S. support of a coalition of political parties led by Herbert Blaize succeeded in establishing a government that clearly identified with U.S. interests. However, the victorious coalition was soon divided internally, resulting in the resignation of several ministers and the emergence of a new political force with the potential capability to compete both with Blaize and with the remnants of the New Jewel Movement and Eric Gairy's party. In the meantime, however, in spite of efforts to convert the island into a model of development adhering to the "industrialization by invitation" strategy, economic difficulties have intensified, with repercussions within the Organization of Eastern Caribbean States (OECS), of which Grenada is a member.

In summary, despite U.S. financial assistance through USAID and the National Endowment for Democracy, and despite the political stability achieved initially by the New National Party (NNP) coalition, Grenada is facing new difficulties. The NNP has broken up into its original components: the Grenada National Party (GNP) led by the current prime minister, Herbert Blaize; George Brizan's New Democratic Party; and Francis Alexis' Grenada Democratic Movement. The latter two have withdrawn from the government and initiated active opposition. Other dissidents have joined them and contributed to diminishing by three benches the 12 to 3 advantage that the NNP formerly enjoyed in Parliament. This restructuring of forces, however, not only threatens the continuity of the Blaize government, but also fuels increasing fears that the deposed Eric Gairy could be rehabilitated, or that certain Marxist groups could be revived. Such reasoning caused Blaize to assume extraordinary powers and declare a state of emergency in the country in late 1987. These measures were anticipated by both Brizan and Alexis, who had no sooner abandoned their government posts than they warned of the possibility of increased government repression against opposition groups. They also criticized the government's economic policy, its fiscal policy, increased unemployment, and the country's rapidly deteriorating education and roadways systems.[11]

In the case of Trinidad and Tobago, despite its relatively autonomous foreign policy—clearly evidenced by the critical position taken by this state during the Grenada invasion of 1983—the government of the People's National Movement (PNM), founded by the late Eric Williams, has not entered into open conflict with U.S. interests in the region. Trinidad and Tobago has traditionally adhered to the principle of nonintervention and for this reason, during the Grenada crisis it became momentarily alienated within CARICOM. It had achieved a markedly influential role in that organization as a result of its increased oil income and economic expansion during the 1970s. Trinidad and Tobago's autonomous position was reinforced by an official visit by a Cuban delegation to Port of Spain in November 1983; the agreements signed by both countries on that occasion did not, however, materialize.[12]

Trinidad and Tobago's position, though not necessarily aligned with the socialist bloc, has served to shield the country from the effects of the militarization process that other states in the region have experienced. It did, however, request U.S. military aid in order to stifle a Black Power rebellion during the so-called February Revolution of 1970.

Trinidad and Tobago's relative autonomy from the influence of U.S. foreign policy is the result of its aspirations to CARICOM leadership, reinforced by the economic assistance it was able to offer the community during the 1970s and early 1980s because of its oil income. Despite the subsequent economic crisis, this policy was upheld by the new coalition that succeeded the thirty-year-old regime of the People's National Movement.

Soon after taking oath, A.N.R. Robinson, the new prime minister of Trinidad and Tobago, was forced to deal with the consequences of administrative corruption that had existed during the PNM years. Moreover, he inherited a crisis economy, following the fall in oil prices, and increasing labor and racial tensions, which began to threaten his own government coalition.

In Barbados, the situation has undergone remarkable fluctuations. During the government of Prime Minister Tom Adams, the country endeavored to strengthen its ties with the United States, both at the economic level through the "industrialization by invitation" strategy, based on the inflow of U.S. capital and expansion of the tourism sector, and at the political level, by converting Barbados into the beachhead for U.S. militarization in the region. This militarization process led to the progressive growth of the Barbadian armed forces—with an increase in military spending from BDS $3.5 million in the period 1970–1976 to BDS $73 million in 1976–1983[13]—and to a greater involvement in the political life of neighboring countries (St. Vincent in 1979, Dominica in 1981, and St. Lucia in 1982),[14] culminating in the military intervention in Grenada.

In spite of identification with U.S. interests, the Barbadian economy, traditionally characterized by stability and constant growth as a result of tourist flows, began to experience the difficulties caused by the world recession. Tourism fell by 5 percent in 1981 and 17 percent in 1982, a situation that, together with low sugar prices and the shutdown of some U.S. factories, led to negative economic growth for the first time in two decades. Meanwhile, the Adams strategy of converting Barbados into an "international business center," where banks, insurance companies, and manufacturers enjoy tax exemptions and cheap labor, did not yield the expected results.

In 1984, increased unemployment at 18.3 percent, the highest in a decade, was accompanied by only a 2.9 percent growth and by a substantial increase in taxes, imposed to remedy the country's economic difficulties.[15]

Errol Barrow's Democratic Labour Party (DLP) victory in May 1986 occurred against this background. It opened up new expectations, based on promises to reduce substantially both unemployment and taxes. One year after his victory, Barrow was among the English-speaking Caribbean leaders to enjoy the greatest popular support. He maintained a consistent foreign policy characterized by nonalignment, support for regional integration, and political pragmatism based on the need for political autonomy in the regional framework, while not overlooking the electoral fraud in Guyana or its docile submission to the United States. This policy was clearly expressed during the Seventh CARICOM Summit Conference in July 1986, where Barrow stressed the need to convert the Caribbean into a peace zone, and where he stated that as long as he was prime minister of Barbados, his country's territory "would not be used to intimidate any of its neighbors, whether it be Cuba or the United States of America."[16]

These positions adopted by the more developed CARICOM countries and Grenada were associated with a significant reorientation of the foreign policy of OECS states. In this regard, Grenada's revolutionary experience served to spark joint action to contain the dissemination of its influence throughout the Eastern Caribbean. This was evidenced by the signing of a regional security agreement that excluded Grenada in 1982. The agreement served the additional purpose of providing Eastern Caribbean troops for the U.S. occupation forces in October 1983, together with contingents from Jamaica and Barbados. The position taken by the prime minister of Dominica, Eugenia Charles, in support of the invasion, was shared by most of the other OECS governments. Among these was Montserrat, a British associate state, which participated in the military intervention and was reprimanded by the British government. However, in the aftermath of the intervention and despite substantial economic aid supplied by the United States to Grenada, dissident voices were known to question the creation of a regional security force, which was strongly promoted by the prime minister of Barbados, Tom Adams.

By the close of the 1980s, relative stability reigned in the Eastern Caribbean states, despite political problems in Antigua caused by succession disputes among the sons of Prime Minister Vere Bird and by the opposition's repeated revelations of corruption scandals. An initiative has been advanced to further the process toward a subregional political union in the form of a federation. This federation, which would eventually include Barbados, is being promoted both by James "Sonny" Mitchell, a moderate, in St. Vincent and by conservatives such as Eugenia Charles of Dominica and John Compton of St. Lucia. Compton, however, has also been affected by the repercussions of an Irangate-related scandal involving state-owned St. Lucia aircraft in the transport of weapons to the South Africa–supported UNITA guerrillas in Angola. The DLP government in Barbados, despite the recent death of Barrow, seems amenable to the subregional integration initiative, and willing to overlook the frustration of previous attempts. Antigua has shown itself to be skeptical, while Grenada is looking inward at its own internal strife. Some opposition parties in the region have expressed disagreement and insist on popular consultation, perhaps through a referendum. Even so, the measure would seem to be expedient, if based on progressive intensification of the "functional cooperation" already achieved at the political and economic levels through the founding of the OECS. This achievement reflects a transformation in the secessionist attitudes of some of the smaller islands whose interests are often in contradiction with the CARICOM MDCs. The political and economic viability of the Eastern Caribbean island states is constantly threatened by their limited economic resources and by their limited capacity for autonomous political insertion in the international scene, despite active involvement in international organizations.

The marked dependence of these states on U.S. economic and military aid makes it difficult for them to assume an independent position vis-à-vis U.S. interests in the region, even though CBI benefits have not met their expectations. Moreover, since the Grenada crisis, Great Britain's influence has diminished, while economic ties and recourse to the Lomé III agreement are still a decisive influence in the Eastern Caribbean economies.

The harmonization of this Eastern Caribbean process with the foreign policy shift of some CARICOM MDCs, specifically Jamaica and Guyana, shows a clear tendency toward the consolidation of economic and political ties with the United States, in a process that some analysts have not hesitated to call "Finlandization" of the Caribbean.[17] The more independent policies adopted by Barbados and Trinidad and Tobago do not indicate a clear break with this pattern, and it seems hardly threatened by Michael Manley's recent victory in the Jamaican elections or a return to a PUP government in Belize.

The Netherlands Antilles and Suriname

The 1954 constitution of the Kingdom of the Netherlands established a Tripartite Kingdom, including Holland, the Netherlands Antilles, and Suriname, in which all were equal partners, regardless of the fact that the latter two are highly dependent upon the economic assistance of the former. In the 1980s, this institutional situation changed drastically, following the long period of stability that had been interrupted only by the popular uprising in Curazao in 1969 and by the achievement of Suriname's political independence in 1975, though both countries continued to receive substantial economic assistance from Holland.

In 1986, the aspiration of Aruba to obtain separate status from the Federation of the Netherlands Antilles was granted and this island, now autonomous of the federation, established direct ties with its metropolitan center as part of a process of gradual decolonization designed to lead to independence ten years later. This process developed in the context of an incipient economic crisis, caused by the closing of Exxon's Lago refinery on the island, and a significant popular movement that removed the People's Electoral Movement—the main promoter of "separate status"—from government, replacing it with a coalition headed by the AVP and the Aruban Patriotic Party.[18]

The withdrawal of Aruba from the Federation of the Netherlands Antilles occurred simultaneously with a growing economic crisis in Curazao, the traditional mainstay of the federation, which had been adversely affected by the international economic situation. Practically all economic activity on the island suffered, including tourism, offshore financing activities, trade, and oil refining. The last industry was particularly affected by the proposed shutdown of a Shell refinery whose operation was ultimately taken over by Venezuela, after an agreement was reached with Holland and the Netherlands Antilles. Even so, the social democratic Antiyas Novo movement once again won the elections in 1985, after a one-year government by a Christian democratic party, the National United People's Party.[19]

These events forced both islands, awaiting political independence, to look outward toward the region, notwithstanding the fact that their principal ties, both economic and political, were to be found in the Netherlands. This shift toward the region opened the doors for rapprochement—in the first place, with Venezuela, which has acquired increasing economic and political influence over both islands, and to a lesser extent, with CARICOM. It should be noted, however, that U.S. corporations maintain significant economic involvement, although a general tendency can be identified for foreign investors to abandon these two Dutch islands and for Dutch economic interests to continue to predominate.

The small windward islands—St. Maarten, Saba, and St. Eustatius—which are part of the Federation of the Netherlands Antilles, also have serious problems. Saba and St. Eustatius have shared in the economic prosperity of St. Maarten, whose principal sources of income are tourism and trade. However, Claude Wathey, the leader of the ruling Democratic party in the Dutch part of the island, has expressed the desire to advance toward independence, without, however, being burdened by ties to the remaining islands in the federation.[20]

A more complex situation existed in Suriname until the late 1980s. This former Dutch continental territory gained its independence in 1975, while maintaining its parliamentary political system and continuing to receive substantial economic assistance from the Netherlands. In February 1980, a military coup from the ranks of noncommissioned army officers led to the rise to power of a group of sergeants, who imposed a government known for its political and ideological contradictions and disputes. After numerous internal changes, commander Desi Bouterse began to emerge as the strongman. The successive changes and shifts put into effect by Bouterse, including the execution of fifteen opposition leaders in December 1982, caused Holland to cut off its financial assistance. The United States also eyed the Surinamese government warily, to the extent that it contemplated the possibility of taking measures similar to those implemented in Grenada.

The withdrawal of Dutch assistance was a hard blow to the Surinamese economy at a time when both bauxite production and exports, a determining factor in the country's economic growth, had been decreasing since 1978. The hydroelectric project on the Kabalebo River, designed to provide energy for industrial development, was also delayed. Exports of crops such as rice and sugar continue to be limited.

The combination of advisory services to the military by members of the radical left, an intensifying nonaligned position, and rapprochement with Cuba, Grenada, and Nicaragua seemed, in 1983, to indicate a definite socialist orientation on the part of the Bouterse government. However, this was not translated into concrete measures that would affect the control of bauxite production by the Alcoa and Billiton companies.

The U.S. occupation of Grenada marked the end of the leftist adventure. Cuban ambassador Oswaldo Cárdenas and the bulk of the powerful Cuban embassy in Paramaribo were asked to leave. Links with Nicaragua were rapidly dissolved and new actors began to take a more active role in the Surinamese scene, among them Brazil. The shift, however, did not change the attitude of the United States or the Netherlands, which persisted in demanding the initiation of a democratization process in Suriname. Bowing to pressure, Bouterse began to negotiate with the sectors and political parties he had displaced in 1980, in an effort to determine the necessary steps for a return to democracy.

In this process, a new factor contributed to speeding up the road to democracy. In late 1986, a guerrilla offensive, led by a former Bouterse bodyguard and supported by Holland-based exiles, began to take shape along the French Guiana border area. Initial steps taken by Bouterse to seek Libyan aid resulted in French support to the rebels. Guerrilla operations and isolation of part of the territory from Paramaribo forced a temporary shutdown of some bauxite-producing centers during 1987 and exacerbated the slump in the Surinamese economy.

Democratization nevertheless proceeded and elections were held in 1987, with highly favorable results for the traditional political parties that had been removed from power in 1980. As a result of negotiations, certain aspects of government were left in military hands, thus excluding the possibility of bringing to trial those who had participated in the coup. Under these conditions, Holland and the United States began to restructure their relations with Suriname and active involvement by Brazil and Venezuela also commenced. The prospects for economic recovery in the short term, however, seemed bleak.[21]

On the regional scene, Aruba and the Netherlands Antilles have expressed their intention of joining CARICOM at some point in the future and Suriname has tried insistently to join since the mid-1970s. Suriname has been admitted as observer, together with the Dominican Republic and Haiti, until such time as the member states decide on its accession.

Haiti and the Dominican Republic

The Haitian situation is unique in the island Caribbean. In the first place, Haiti has earned some of the most dramatic statistics in the region: it has the lowest per capita income in the hemisphere and the highest illiteracy rate. Its political history, begun in 1804 with the founding of the first black republic in the world, has been tainted, first, by the U.S. occupation in the early twentieth century, which lasted until 1933 and, second, by the consolidation of power of the repressive Duvalier dynasty, founded in 1957. In the years following the fleeing of "Baby Doc" in February 1986, the country faced a serious political crisis.

A junta set up by General Namphy after Duvalier's exit was initially taken to be a sign of improvement in the unstable political climate that weighed heavily over Haiti. But, in the following two years, during the debate on the democratization process and approval of the new constitution, a clear polarization began to emerge between the armed forces and the Duvalier camp, on the one hand, and a wide range of personalities, political parties, religious and human rights organizations, and community organizations, on the other. The pressures on the junta, exerted mainly by popular action and frequently spearheaded by Catholic Church figures, continued to intensify. The political opposition embodied in the parties was, however, fragmented and dispersed, resulting in the nomination of over one hundred presidential candidates during the months leading to the November 1987 elections.

In the meantime, the economy continued to deteriorate beyond even the dramatic situation left by Jean-Claude Duvalier, and the junta was unable to formulate a coherent policy during the impasse. Assistance from the United States, Canada, and the European Community did not relieve the situation, in a country where administrative corruption and misuse of public funds had become part of the local political culture. Faced with the heterogeneous political forces and presidential candidates, the United States did not venture to offer sufficient economic support, although it had expressed the will to prevent chaos from taking hold of the country and fostering the rise to power of radical popular forces.

During this period, many teams of political analysts from various states in the region, ranging from CARICOM to the two major political parties in

Venezuela, visited Haiti to study the situation and support the democratization process. The delegations trekked through Haiti while violence and political disorder reigned. Finally, during the elections of 29 November 1987, the junta interrupted the Electoral Council and suspended the proceedings, with the pretext that irregularities and a general climate of instability and violence rendered a normal electoral process impossible. Four of the candidates who, according to foreign observers, had the strongest popular support, formed an opposition coalition that boycotted the new call to elections in January 1988. In spite of a high rate of abstention, the elections were carried out and won by the candidate of the Rassemblement Democratique, Leslie Manigat.

Reactions came swiftly, with many critics pointing to the support this candidate had managed to receive from the junta. Canada has questioned the validity of an election in which less than 20 percent of the electorate voted. France too has been critical of the results of the January elections, but Venezuela was supportive of the new president-elect. The Socialist International and the Christian Democratic Organization of America (ODCA) also supported Manigat.

The greatest range of opinions prevailed within CARICOM, where the most extreme positions were those of the governments of Jamaica and Dominica on the one hand, supporting the January electoral process, and Trinidad and Tobago and Barbados, on the other hand, which challenged it.[22]

Haiti's political instability and economic crisis are regarded as a threat by neighboring Dominican Republic, where a further deterioration of the Haitian crisis, already aggravated by the involvement of military sectors in drug trafficking, could lead to a greater influx of Haitian migrants.

The democratic stability established in 1978 in Dominican Republic with the electoral victory of the Democratic Revolutionary Party (PRD) was threatened, as we have seen, by successive political crises within the party and government. This crisis situation strongly contributed in May 1986 to the presidential re-election of Joaquín Balaguer, who had maintained a stable government in the period following U.S. intervention in 1965. Despite significant economic growth in 1987, even if the Dominican Republic refused an IMF agreement, and an intensified campaign against administrative corruption and illicit earnings, the situation nonetheless degenerated in late 1988, with special consequences for the less privileged sectors. Thus, in contrast to the economic stabilization achieved in 1987 with a sizable increase in tourist flows and growing industrial development in the free zones, 1988 was marked by an increase in social and political tensions. Strikes and popular action, usually led by the National Confederation of People's Organizations (CNOP), were numerous.[23]

The opposition, in turn, composed of the Democratic Revolutionary Party (PRD), still trying to recover from the internal conflicts and accusations of corruption that plagued its term of government, and the Dominican

Liberation Party, headed by Juan Bosch, was unable to put together an active policy with which to oppose the government and, instead, was displaced by the action of community-based groups.

The Balaguer government attempted to diversify its economic relations, establishing, for example, a preferential agreement with the European Community similar to the Lomé agreement for the ACP group.

In this general context, it should be borne in mind that, especially since the Cuban revolution, the bulk of U.S. military aid to Caribbean states has been concentrated in Haiti and the Dominican Republic, though in the case of Haiti, the political events of 1988 and increased involvement of military sectors in drug trafficking have caused a suspension in U.S. military assistance.

Historical tensions between Haiti and the Dominican Republic have been exacerbated by U.S. assistance aimed mainly at consolidating counterinsurgency activities of both armed forces. Suffice it to say that in Haiti, the armed forces are composed of 7,600 men out of a population of 5,632,000 inhabitants, while in the Dominican Republic, out of 6,434,000 inhabitants, 21,365 men were serving in the armed forces as of 1930–1961.[24] To this must be added that in both the Dominican Republic, since the time of the Trujillo dictatorship, and in Haiti as well, despite circumstances causing divergence with the Duvalier family, the military have exercised significant political influence.

The French Overseas Departments

Regionalization efforts implemented by the Mitterrand government as of 1981 gave rise to a new administrative and organizational level in the form of a regional council, which mediates between the overseas departments and the central government. This measure, which followed the 1946 departmentalization, may eventually convert St. Martin and St. Barthelemy into autonomous territories of Guadeloupe.[25]

This process falls within the general trend toward a greater degree of autonomy for the DOMs, a trend currently promoted by both the central government and a considerable portion of the representative sectors of the islands. Indeed, even those groups that tend to be most in favor of independence have tended in recent times to propose a greater degree of autonomy for the departments, without, however, seeking political independence from France. A major consideration operating here is the possibility of suspension of metropolitan economic assistance in the event of independence. French assistance has accounted for the DOMS status among the territories with the highest standard of living in the region.[26] This privileged status will soon be reinforced by the fact that the elimination of borders in the European Community, to occur in 1992, will include the French Overseas Departments.

Both Guadeloupe and Martinique have nevertheless tended to establish varying types of ties with neighboring Caribbean countries, with the support of France, which recently established an embassy in St. Lucia to serve the Eastern Caribbean.

From the strategic point of view, it is vital to France to maintain control over the DOMS, regardless of any regionalization measures and despite increasing autonomy in the territories. Without full membership in NATO, France needs to maintain its own operational bases in the Western hemisphere in order to assure access to its Pacific territories. These territories are a crucial link on the route from France to its Mururoa Island atomic test range and are also vital in ensuring strategic development of the aerospace center at Kourou in French Guiana. Reinforcement of the French military garrisons on the two larger islands and in French Guiana and the ongoing economic assistance that has characterized its policy toward the overseas departments can be seen in this light.

In the latter part of the 1980s there were 7,000 French military personnel distributed among the various territories in the region, with two naval support units. Some of these troops have taken part in joint exercises with the United States, the Netherlands, and Brazil, while U.S. counterinsurgency groups have been trained in the French Guiana jungles.[27]

Carrying out joint exercises with the United States, however, does not imply full convergence of objectives in the region. Two members of the French military recently pointed out that "Il ne s'agit pas, pour l'Europe . . . de contrebalancer l'action américaine, mais de jouer le rôle de tampon entre la puissance des Etats Unis et la susceptibilité des Etats Caraibes, à la fin de contenir l'expansion cubaine."[28]

In Guadeloupe, while pro-independence groups lack popular backing and have to a certain extent been reduced, their position was reinforced by the Communist Party decision in the late 1980s to adopt a pro-independence stance, which constituted a clear break with the socialists.[29] This decision, combined with a significant increase in DOM unemployment and prevailing tensions between the local population and French residents, may give rise to a new surge in pro-independence activities owing to the impact of New Caledonian political events.

U.S. Policy in the Caribbean

From the beginning of the nineteenth century, the United States explicitly established a policy of southward expansion of its borders. This policy reached a climax in the 1846–1848 Mexican War, resulting in the annexation of part of Mexico's territory. The so-called two-hemisphere doctrine, together with the Monroe Doctrine, reflected U.S. ambitions of hegemony in the

Western Hemisphere, formulated as a "manifest destiny."[30] Between 1803 and 1853, in just half a century, the United States expanded its territory from the thirteen original colonies to practically all of its present territory, mostly at the expense of Latin America.

It was not until 1895, however, when U.S. attention was focused on Central America and the Caribbean, that this policy took its most blatant form. Beginning with the Spanish-American War in 1898 and until 1965, the United States intervened directly over fifteen times in Cuba, Haiti, the Dominican Republic, and Puerto Rico (ultimately annexing it to the United States),[31] and carried out a similar number of interventions in Central America as well. At the same time, it exercised increasing influence in the rest of the continent. Throughout this process, the United States sought to achieve three long-term objectives in Latin America, which were related to the concepts underlying the Monroe Doctrine: (1) to prevent and eventually eliminate all influence of nonhemispheric actors; (2) to ensure its own leadership in the Western Hemisphere and direct control in the Caribbean; and (3) to develop political stability in the Latin American states in order to guarantee the preceding objective.[32]

The forms of direct domination established in Central America and the Caribbean were thus clearly differentiated from the forms of hegemony developed in South America, which some analysts have euphemistically termed "relevant influence."[33]

The "gunboat diplomacy" phase, an offshoot of the Roosevelt corollary to the Monroe Doctrine, with its emphasis on the United States' watchdog role, and the "dollar diplomacy" launched during the Taft administration as a means for defending the economic interests of U.S. private sector investments in Latin America, were followed, beginning in 1929, by the so-called "good neighbor policy." Within the framework of this policy, military intervention as a political instrument was abandoned and thus, by 1936, the chapter of U.S. occupation in Cuba, Haiti, the Dominican Republic, Nicaragua, and Panama was momentarily closed.[34]

In developments parallel to this historical process, the sharing of hemispheric hegemony between the United States and Great Britain, which had characterized the period between 1822 and 1901, came to an end in 1903 with the signing of the Hay-Bunau-Varilla Treaty establishing perpetual U.S. control of the Panama Canal.[35] During the course of the first half of the century, Great Britain limited its influence in the region to its colonial territories; British ties with South America also persisted, though they changed considerably after World War II.

Once U.S. influence was guaranteed in the Central American and Hispanic Caribbean subregion, the latter became associated with the rest of Latin America in the framework of the Pan American policies set out for the hemisphere. Thus, from the U.S. perspective, the Hispanic Caribbean was associated with Latin America, while the rest of the Caribbean territories remained linked to the European colonial powers still present in the region. (Denmark withdrew from the region after the U.S. purchase of the Virgin Islands in 1917.)

Reconsideration of the subregion in U.S. hemispheric policy as clearly distinct from the rest of Latin America first occurred during the Carter administration.[36] During the second half of the 1970s, after various significant political events, the Caribbean Basin began to emerge as a subregion with its own characteristics. First, the Cuban revolutionary government had consolidated its authority and increased its interest in the area, which was expressed in a specific regional policy; second, the postcolonial, non-Hispanic Caribbean states had emerged as specific actors in the region; and third, with the ripening of the political crisis in Central America, the Sandinista government established itself in Nicaragua after accomplishing the downfall of Somoza. Although these processes had begun to take shape in the preceding decade, they did not actually come together until the 1970s, at that point the strategic importance of the Caribbean Basin was revitalized on the basis of geopolitical interests. It was in this context that the State Department arrived at the Caribbean Basin concept.[37]

Despite the significance granted historically by the United States to the subregion, during this period its strategic importance was highlighted principally from the point of view of a possible armed conflict in Europe, which would require NATO forces to be supplied through the area. To quote Sheila Harden:

> Put at its most extreme, one element of nuclear strategy envisages an East-West war beginning with a land battle of limited duration in Europe. It is argued that if such a land battle is to remain non-nuclear for an acceptable period, then material and supplies must be able to pass swiftly and unimpeded from the United States through the deep water channels between the Caribbean islands to Europe.[38]

In practice, the region links four areas that are important from the strategic viewpoint: the United States, Western Europe, West Africa, and the Persian Gulf.[39]

From the point of view of still other geopolitical considerations, the "domino theory" proposes that the spread of revolutionary phenomena, such as the Nicaraguan case, in the whole of Central America and the insular Caribbean could affect stability in Mexico and, therefore, U.S. security. From the strategic point of view, it is also vital for the United States to maintain control of the Panama Canal, particularly in the eyes of U.S. public opinion.[40]

By the same token, various geopolitical criteria reinforce U.S. concern for a region considered to be its "backyard." Important oil refineries have been established in the Virgin Islands, Puerto Rico, Trinidad, Venezuela, and the Bahamas and moreover, most U.S. oil imports are shipped through the Gulf of Mexico and the Caribbean. Furthermore, half of U.S. bauxite and aluminum imports come from the region, as well as one-twelfth of its nickel consumption.[41] A good portion of all these products must cross the Caribbean Basin in order to reach the United States and thus, control of the area is a vital element in defending strategic U.S. interests.

To the above general picture must be added the existence of substantial U.S. investment in the Caribbean, as mentioned in previous sections; a large U.S. community in the various Caribbean countries; and, significantly, the constant, albeit frequently illegal, flow of migration to the United States. For all of these reasons, the Caribbean Basin is highly important to the United States.

Jimmy Carter, who was the first U.S. president to consider the Caribbean subregion in intrinsic terms, beyond the East-West conflict, initiated a series of economic assistance measures that were at first characterized by cooperation and multilateralism.[42] This policy was not unrelated to the manifest economic interests of the United States in the region and to the human factors linked to the extensive migration from the Caribbean to its northern neighbor; however, it was more fundamentally tied to U.S. strategic and geopolitical interests,[43] despite the relative stabilization that had been achieved in the region during the preceding decade and throughout the 1970s. The Carter administration initially focused its concern on the socioeconomic situation in the region, following the guidelines established early on in the aid programs for the Caribbean Basin. Consequently, regional policy was governed by five principles repeatedly set out by Carter administration spokespersons:

1. Significant support for economic development;
2. Firm commitment to democratic practices and human rights;
3. Clear acceptance of ideological pluralism;
4. Unequivocal respect for national sovereignty; and
5. Strong encouragement of regional cooperation and of an active Caribbean role in world affairs.[44]

These principles were harmonized with several specific Carter administration objectives: a redefinition of alliances with other developed capitalized countries within the Trilateral Commission; stabilization of the international situation in favor of détente and arms limitation; and encouragement and promotion of ideological, political, and economic means of influence vis-à-vis the Third World.[45] Furthermore, an improvement in relations with Cuba and the signing of agreements with Panama whereby the Panama Canal would revert to Panama in the year 2000 contributed to giving the early years of the Carter administration's regional policy a "positive" image.[46]

In general terms, this first phase of Carter's Caribbean Basin policy was noted for its use of nonmilitary foreign policy instruments, combined with limited military activity in the region, and diplomacy that stressed human rights and political and social pluralism.[47]

By 1979, this orientation had shifted dramatically. Increasing Cuban military activity in Ethiopia and the crisis originating with the presence of a Soviet brigade in Cuba in September 1979 caused a substantial change in relations between Washington and Havana.[48]

Moreover, the establishment of the Sandinista government in Nicaragua and the rise to power of a radical government in Grenada, after the successful coup against Eric Gairy, also contributed to a general picture that the United States regarded as a threat to its interests. To this was added the taking of U.S. hostages in Iran, which caused a drastic shift in Carter's human rights stance and led to a more aggressive subregional policy.

Once again, U.S. security interests began to be emphasized in regional policy, which was thereafter perceived fundamentally in the light of East-West confrontation. The region was redefined as a geopolitical unit and the first steps toward its militarization were taken with the creation of the U.S. Forces Caribbean Command, which included a Caribbean Task Force based in Key West, naval forces stationed in Puerto Rico (the Antilles Defense Command), and army, air force, and marine corps units.[49]

The advent of the Reagan administration in the United States led to an even narrower definition of this policy in terms of global confrontation with the USSR, justifying the new president's more aggressive attitude toward containment of Soviet interests. In fact, the region began to be regarded as a U.S. foreign policy priority of vital importance, as in the days of the Monroe Doctrine.[50] To quote Maingot:

> Carter tended to see the insular Caribbean as a discreet entity for policy purposes; Reagan's new emphasis on the "Caribbean Basin," by linking the islands with Central America, has tended to make into one what has always been and continues to be two quite distinct realities. The fundamental difference, however, has been in the use of diplomacy, including very importantly the official style and language of that diplomacy.[51]

The new administration's ideological emphasis adhered to the proposals of the new right in the United States and its desire that the country take a more aggressive role in the direction of world affairs in order to avoid isolation. It was also in line with the new right's undisguised view that communism was the foremost threat to U.S. interests, that its spread must consequently be prevented, and that expansion of its principal promoter, the Soviet Union, must at all costs be restricted.[52] Consonant with these postulates and despite differences between the situation of the Central American countries and that of the island Caribbean, the region was dealt with as a unit of fundamental strategic importance, thus taking to extremes a concept that had begun to be formulated under different conditions during the previous administration. Cuba became the principal objective of regional policy and was perceived as an extension of Soviet interests in the Caribbean, as well as the source of inspiration and support for revolutionary processes in Nicaragua and Grenada. It was from this perspective that the security objective and its corollary, U.S. prestige vis-à-vis the conflict with the USSR, were given top priority; the "low-intensity conflict" policy was adopted, which was intended to further containment of the Soviets without leading to direct confrontation.[53]

As a result of this policy, coupled with the accelerated militarization process to reaffirm the U.S. presence in the area, numerous covert and counterinsurgency operations were undertaken.[54] The internal crisis unleashed within the government of the New Jewel Movement in Grenada and the subsequent military occupation was probably the best opportunity that could have offered itself to the Reagan administration for reaffirming U.S. hegemony in the region, an action incurring relatively low military costs, but paying high political and psychological dividends. The occupation of Grenada allowed the United States to neutralize leftist sectors in the region, to isolate Cuba in the island Caribbean, and to promote certain governments, such as those of Jamaica and Barbados, which at the time identified openly with U.S. policy.

Puerto Rico played a fundamental role in the regional militarization process within the context of an "indirect confrontation" policy toward Cuba, a policy that led both to a strengthening of the U.S. military presence and to increased military capacity of the armed forces and police of other states in the region to guarantee Caribbean security.[55] Besides allowing an operational base for extensive naval maneuvers initiated in 1981, the Puerto Rican role made it possible for the United States to expand military facilities and bases in the area, to train police forces of the Caribbean Basin states by using the Puerto Rican National Guard in various ways, and generally to increase the U.S. presence in the Eastern Caribbean. Puerto Rican society itself underwent a significant militarization process and became the operational base for launching the Grenada invasion, as well as its strategic rear guard.[56] A subsequent report by the Puerto Rico Lawyers' Association denounced activities aimed at turning the Roosevelt Roads naval base into a command center for the control of nuclear weapons, in open violation of the Tlatelolco Treaty.[57]

At this stage, the bulk of U.S. military assistance was sent to the Dominican Republic and Jamaica and, in the Eastern Caribbean, to Barbados.[58]

French and Dutch troops stationed in their respective territories participated in NATO maneuvers at the regional level. Great Britain also contributed to the training and supply of police forces in the Eastern Caribbean, in coordination with the United States after the Grenada intervention.

Cuban Policy Toward the Region

It was not until the mid-1970s that Cuba began to project a specific policy in respect to the non-Hispanic Caribbean. During the previous decade, Cuba had concentrated on its support to guerrilla movements on the mainland as a significant aspect of its foreign policy and had therefore exercised a definitely "Latin Americanist" bias. The failure of these guerrilla efforts led to a reformulation of the Cuban position, which was thereafter aimed, among other objectives, at establishing links with those governments in the region that showed a progressive or nationalistic leaning. The new objectives also included projection of Cuba in Africa as part of a new global perspective, which policy gave rise in the second half of the 1970s to active Cuban involvement in Angola and Ethiopia.[59]

Within this framework, Cuba increased its participation in the Movement of Non-Aligned Countries and reinforced its regional presence, particularly with respect to independent English-speaking states, by means of technical assistance and cultural exchange programs. In addition, Cuba established political ties with progressive parties in the Caribbean states. The beginning of this process was marked by the visit of Fidel Castro to Georgetown in September 1973, where he met with the prime ministers of Guyana, Trinidad, Barbados, and Jamaica. Castro's visit was followed by a visit to Havana by Prime Minister Eric Williams of Trinidad and Tobago in June 1975; the setting up of political, economic, and cultural ties with Jamaica during Michael Manley's second term in government; a visit by Fidel Castro to Jamaica in 1977; and the strengthening of ties with Grenada in 1979 and with Guyana, through a visit by Burnham to Havana. Fidel Castro's statement in 1975 that Cuba was an Afro-Latin American country was a landmark in this process and led to the projection of the Cuban image in the non-Hispanic Caribbean as an "Afro-Latin State."[60] The appointment of black ambassadors to CARICOM countries, together with an active cultural policy initiated by Cuban participation in Guyana's Carifesta 1972, also contributed to the image of Cuba as different from the rest of Latin America. These policies challenged existing stereotypes of Cuba among the English-speaking states and underlined Cuba's Caribbean ethnocultural image, which was further consolidated by subsequent cultural encounters and exchanges.[61]

The launching of the new Cuban diplomacy in the area was reinforced by the decision by non-Hispanic states to strengthen ties with Cuba, in the context of their own objectives of regional integration, diversification of international relations and, in the long run, containment of local leftist sectors. For Cuba, these developments meant the beginning of a turnaround from OAS-imposed isolation.[62] In practice, the establishment of ties—particularly with Jamaica and Guyana and, to a lesser extent, Trinidad and Tobago—focused on technical cooperation and cultural exchange. Cuban assistance to Jamaica involved sending medical staff; participation in various development projects for roadways infrastructure and construction of public buildings and schools; advisory services in transport, agriculture, and fisheries; and various educational assistance programs, including scholarships for Jamaican students. Similar programs were set up for Guyana, including development projects to assist in fisheries, public health, civil aviation, and education, as well as a program for supplying cement. In the case of Trinidad and Tobago, technical cooperation agreements were signed.[63]

The identification of common ethnohistorical characteristics as the mainstay for a policy of rapprochement with the non-Hispanic Caribbean led to the creation of a positive image for the revolutionary process in the region, an image strengthened by Cuba's progress in the area of public health and in the struggle against poverty, illiteracy, and unemployment—issues that have traditionally plagued non-Hispanic Caribbean societies.[64] This new image allowed Cuba to project itself effectively in the Caribbean region, supported mainly by technical cooperation programs but also by some trade agreements. The process was reinforced by the evolution of the revolutionary experiment in Grenada, where Cuban assistance was offered in similar areas, notably in the construction of the Point Salines airport.

This state policy was harmonized with a rapprochement between the Cuban Communist Party and progressive and nationalist political parties in the English-speaking states, whether or not they identified with Marxist ideology.[65] In the cases of Grenada, Guyana, and Suriname, military advisers and training were provided.

In general terms, throughout the 1970s, Cuban policy grounded its political and ideological strategy for rapprochement with the non-Hispanic Caribbean—including some conservative governments—on a shared identity, derived from a common ethnocultural base and differentiated only by language and the various metropolitan cultural traditions. Cuba's closest ties, however, were established with Michael Manley in Jamaica and Maurice Bishop in Grenada.

These steps taken by the Cuban government during the 1970s, combined with occasional support from Caribbean states in international forums, made it possible for Cuba to reverse its regional isolation and to identify with the region so as to offset U.S. pressure. The measures also allowed Cuba to set out its own regional policy objectives—which were not always identical to those of the USSR—without having to forgo its support of revolutionary movements and parties and without having to set aside its objectives of international solidarity. Within this framework, Cuba stimulated a nationalist boom in the region, which led to a weakening of U.S. influence and which fully coincided with the Soviet Union's global policy objectives.

Although Fidel Castro's defense objectives were aimed at guaranteeing the revolutionary process vis-à-vis the United States and obtaining sufficient levels of assistance so as to promote development of the island, he also hoped to make Cuba increasingly autonomous in its condition as a USSR client-state and to ensure his own regional leadership and influence. These objectives were in line with those of the Soviet Union, inasmuch as they worked against U.S. hegemony in the Caribbean Basin, forced the United States to allocate resources to the region that would otherwise have been spent on other regions, and contributed to expanding Soviet power. Castro's desire to increase Cuban autonomy and to consolidate his own influence in the region did not coincide with Soviet objectives, especially at the regional level, a fact that became clearly evident during the Grenadan crisis.[66]

These differences notwithstanding, as of 1960 the Soviet Union helped to consolidate Cuban military strength by providing it with arms, training, and the largest naval fleet in the Caribbean.[67]

However, the Soviet presence, together with the militarization process in Cuban society, reversed the positive image that Cuba had succeeded in building up in the non-Hispanic Caribbean during the preceding years. A high point in this new direction was reached in 1980 when Cuban aircraft attacked a coast guard patrol in the Bahamas, and Cuban advisers began to arrive in Grenada. Both situations were cause for increasing regional concern in regard to Cuban military strength and this, in turn, abruptly eradicated the favorable image achieved in the preceding decade.[68]

The active Cuban presence in Grenada and, to a lesser extent, in Suriname (800 Cuban advisers and construction workers in the former and 100 advisers in the latter) caused conservative governments in the Eastern Caribbean to see before them the specter of the communist threat, at a time when the predominant ideological environment was changing. Indeed, some analysts pointed to subversive "triangles" or "squares" in the region formed by Cuba, Nicaragua, Grenada, and eventually, Suriname.[69] These developments were compounded by significant expansion of the various leftist groupings and parties in the Caribbean and by the consolidation of their regional ties, initiated in the mid-1970s. Another factor operative in this context was the divergence in alignments occurring during the Malvinas/Falklands conflict, which brought into the spotlight a clear dividing line between Latin American and non-Hispanic countries in the hemisphere. To some extent, this too caused a reversal in the process of Cuba's identification as a full member of the Caribbean community.[70]

The U.S. invasion of Grenada was supported by most of the non-Hispanic Caribbean governments, with the exception of Trinidad and Tobago, Guyana, Belize, the Bahamas, and Suriname. It was even regarded with relief by some of the regional powers, despite their public statements defending the principle of nonintervention. For Cuba, however, it marked a decisive setback in its influence over the non-Hispanic Caribbean, both in respect to its regional ties and because it represented a reversal of leftist achievements in general in the Caribbean. In addition to the sudden cooling of relations with Suriname, Marxist parties in the region were strongly divided between, on the one hand, those who identified with the "orthodoxy" promoted by Bernard Coard, and on the other, the more pragmatic followers of Maurice Bishop, who had supported his populist orientation. This division weakened the convergence of both communist and radical parties that had originated in the Black Power movement in the Caribbean, giving rise to a situation which has yet to be overcome.[71]

The Grenadan crisis also revealed Cuba's limited capacity to confront the United States militarily in the region. Moreover, the subsequent campaign in the U.S. press notwithstanding, it also demonstrated existing differences between Cuban and Soviet policy at the regional level. It should be noted, furthermore, that the Soviet military presence in the Caribbean is restricted to its Cuban bases and that the Cuban presence in the region as a whole has progressively diminished.[72]

Since the Grenada invasion, Cuba's position in the region has weakened, despite efforts to reactivate its ties with the non-Hispanic Caribbean. Relations with Trinidad and, after Barrow's victory, with Barbados, are of little significance, while in the cases of Jamaica and Suriname and, to a lesser degree, Guyana, relations have been totally reversed. The only truly active area in Cuba's regional policy at the end of the 1980s was an increase in economic relations with the Dominican Republic.

The Regional Powers

As already observed, Latin American regional powers, particularly Mexico, Colombia, and Venezuela, have developed specific policies toward the region. In the Mexican case, in the late 1970s, its interest in the Caribbean Basin was replaced by a new priority interest in the Pacific Basin. Despite multilateral agreements whereby it participates in the Caribbean Development Bank and the San José Agreement, in the 1980s it was primarily concerned with the Western Caribbean, mainly Jamaica and the Dominican Republic, and with Central America, while its ties with Cuba dating from the 1970s began to wane. Relations with Trinidad and Tobago and Guyana were also substantially reduced, to the extent that the process has been described as an "involution."[73]

Colombia has undergone a similar process. It did not launch an active Caribbean policy until 1981, when it did so as a result of the Betancur government's Third World orientation. During this period, the Caribbean Basin was accorded priority rank in Colombian foreign policy, with an emphasis on the mainland, particularly Central America. Relations with the non-Hispanic Caribbean are practically limited to the Netherlands Antilles. With liberal Virgilio Barco's rise to power and with the new emphasis on economic rather than political priorities, Colombian foreign policy shifted its attention toward the Pacific Basin, as Mexico had already done. Throughout this process, the limited relations with the non-Hispanic Caribbean focused on scientific, technical, and educational cooperation agreements, instead of economic assistance and cooperation.[74]

Paradoxically, both in the Mexican and the Colombian cases, trade relations were more active with Puerto Rico and, to a lesser extent, with the Dominican Republic.

During the last presidential term of office, Venezuelan policy toward the Caribbean was much more active and specific. The appointment of a special ambassador for Caribbean affairs signaled this shift, which was further reinforced by President Jaime Lusinchi's travels to various states in the non-Hispanic Caribbean during 1988. Emphasis has been on cultural exchange agreements, assistance in science and education, and in technical cooperation; however, there have also been numerous incentives for economic activity in the Caribbean, particularly through the private sector. A substantial change has therefore occurred in the traditional pattern of Venezuelan economic assistance, from a policy generally based on providing loans and grants, to the goal of economic cooperation, based on "shared responsibility." Activation of this policy was favored by an improvement in relations with Guyana, when selection of a mechanism for solving the Venezuela-Guyana dispute over the Esequibo border territory was left to the United Nations secretary-general. This circumstance and the cultural policy developed in the late 1980s have led to a significant change in Caribbean perceptions of Venezuela's role in the region.[75]

It should be remembered that, from the geopolitical point of view, various factors exist that cause the region to be particularly important to Venezuela. First, Venezuela's geography is such that a significant portion of the population is concentrated in the 2,256 kilometers of Caribbean coastline. The country's major ports are to be found along this coastline and most of Venezuela's communications with the world at large depend on these port cities. Moreover, 80 percent of Venezuelan exports—especially vital oil exports—must cross this area, as must most imports into the country. Furthermore, the island Caribbean is an important potential market for numerous Venezuelan products, particularly textiles, processed foodstuffs, petrochemical products, and light industry, all of which became singularly relevant when the country sought to replace the "import substitution" model by an "export promotion" model, as a key aspect in its economic development. This changeover was evidenced in the reformulation of economic policy in the wake of the oil crisis and the events of "Black Friday" in February 1983.

Within this framework, Venezuela has partially attained its political objectives in the Caribbean, which are aimed principally at exercising a stabilizing influence in support of its own security interests. Venezuela participated in the reinstatement of the democratic system in Grenada after the 1983 crisis; in the Surinamese democratization process by exercising, together with Brazil, a moderate influence over the Bouterse military government; and it has become actively involved in the democratization process in Haiti. These measures, which are generally in agreement with U.S. policy in the region, are not, however, necessarily indicative of a convergence with the United States on regional political objectives, as is illustrated by the country's involvement in the democratization processes of Suriname and Haiti.

The promotion of democratic systems in the region, a topic that has been especially dear to Venezuelan diplomacy since 1958, has frequently been possible only because Cuba, Venezuela's traditional competitor in the area, is no longer actively present. Venezuelan concern for regional stability in relation to its geopolitical interests has led to participation in the Eastern Caribbean states' military training, particularly in the naval area.

Finally, as already pointed out, it is necessary to take into account a new actor in the non-Hispanic Caribbean, Brazil, which was especially active in Suriname and Guyana, and, in the late 1980s to a lesser extent, in Trinidad and the Eastern Caribbean. Brazilian military assistance to these two non-Hispanic continental states has been a cause of concern to other regional powers inasmuch as it frequently challenges some of the geopolitical postulates formerly expressed by their own armed forces. It is frequently a cause for concern as well during moments of heightened geopolitical competitiveness among the Latin American countries working in the region. A distinctive feature of Brazil's Caribbean policy is that it does not always coincide with U.S. foreign policy guidelines.

From this perspective, it can be said that since the 1970s, there has generally been a trend in the regional powers' Caribbean policies toward greater autonomy vis-à-vis U.S. interests. This trend has been demonstrated by activities of the Contadora and Support Group, where geopolitical priorities are derived from the respective national and regional interests, rather than from alignments imposed by East-West confrontation.

Notes

1. The Resource Center: *Jamaica: Open for Business,* Albuquerque, 1984, p. 11.
2. C. Sunshine: *The Caribbean: Survival, Struggle and Sovereignty,* Washington, D.C.: EPICA, 1985, p. 152.
3. Ibid.
4. See Anthony Payne: "The United States and the Eastern Caribbean Since the Invasion of Grenada," paper presented at the International Colloquium on Eastern Caribbean Geopolitics, Oxford University, January 1988.
5. The Resource Center: *Jamaica,* p. 33.
6. Scott MacDonald: "The Future of Foreign Aid in the Caribbean After

Grenada: Finlandization and Confrontation in the Eastern Tier," *Inter-American Economics Affairs,* 38, 4 (1985), p. 65.

7. Ibid.

8. Henry Gill: "Granada: la política interna y externa de la revolución," in *Gaceta Internacional,* 1, 2 (1983), pp. 138–146.

9. Ibid.

10. For a more detailed analysis of the Grenadan crisis and its consequences, see Serbin, *Etnicidad.*

11. *Caribbean Contact,* August 1987.

12. MacDonald: "The Future of Foreign Aid," p. 69.

13. *Caribbean Contact,* October 1983.

14. In December 1979, the Barbados Defence Forces were directly involved in repressing a Rastafarian group in St. Vincent, in response to an uprising inspired by the Grenadan revolutionary government. This force also aided the government of Dominica in 1981 in putting down a coup attempt; in May 1982, it took up positions along the St. Lucia coastline to guarantee the electoral process that brought conservative John Compton to power.

15. *Caribbean Contact,* 1986.

16. Ibid.

17. See Scott MacDonald: "The Future of Foreign Aid," and Roberto Espíndola: "Security Dilemmas," in *Politics, Security and Development in Small States,* edited by Colin Clarke and Tony Payne, London: Allen and Unwin, 1987.

18. Giacalone: "Antillas Neerlandesas," p. 19.

19. Ibid.

20. Hoetink: "The Windward Islands," p. 3.

21. See Serbin: "Surinam."

22. *Caribbean Insight,* February 1988.

23. *Caribbean Insight,* April 1988.

24. International Institute for Strategic Studies: *The Military Balance,* London: IISS, 1987, pp. 188–191.

25. Girault: "Les Caraibes de l'est," p. 8.

26. Constant: "Décentralisation," p. 17.

27. *Latin American Regional Report-Caribbean,* December 1985.

28. Rebour and Trehard: "Signification strategique de l'espace caraibe," in *Defense Nationale* (April–May 1986), p. 94.

29. *Caribbean Insight,* April 1988.

30. Pope Atkins: *América Latina en el sistema político internacional,* Mexico City: Gernika, 1980, pp. 107–108.

31. Barry et al.: *The Other Side of Paradise,* p. 265.

32. Atkins: "America Latina," pp. 103–104.

33. F. Parkinson: "La crisis centroaméricana," paper presented at the Annual Convention of the British International Studies Association, Aberswyth, December 1987, p. 12.

34. Atkins: "America Latina," pp. 112–114.

35. Idem.

36. Anthony Maingot: "American Foreign Policy in the Caribbean: Continuities, Changes and Contingencies," in *International Journal,* 40 (1985), pp. 320–330.

37. Maingot asserts that this concept is based on an approach outlined by Florida businessmen, while Boersner attributes its origin to policy outlined by the Department of State in the 1970s.

38. Sheila Harden: *Small is Dangerous: Microstates in a Macroworld,* London: Frances Pinter Press, 1985, p. 149.

39. See Marvin Gordon: "The Geopolitics of the Caribbean Basin," *Military Review* (August 1986).

40. In "American Foreign Policy," Maingot emphasizes the importance of the U.S. problem with image and international prestige, as does Sutton, "EEC Development Assistance," and Child, "Issues for U.S. Policy."

41. Jaramillo: "Problemas de seguridad," pp. 86–87.

42. Maingot: "American Foreign Policy," pp. 320–330.

43. See Tony Payne, Paul Sutton, and Tony Thorndike: *Grenada: Revolution and Invasion,* London: Croom Helm, 1984.

44. Ibid., p. 44.

45. Jorge Rodríguez Beruff: "Puerto Rico and the Militarization of the Caribbean," in *Contemporary Marxism,* 10 (1985), p. 70.

46. Michael Erisman: "Colossus Challenged: U.S. Caribbean Policy in the 1980s," in *Colosus Challenged: The Struggle for Caribbean Influence,* edited by Michael Erisman and John Martz, Boulder, Colo.: Westview Press, 1982, p. 6.

47. Rodríguez Beruff: "Puerto Rico and Militarization," p. 71.

48. Idem.

49. Josefina Cintrón Tiryakian: "The Military and Security Dimensions of U.S. Caribbean Policy," in *The Caribbean Challenge: U.S. Policy in a Volatile Region,* edited by Michael Erisman, Boulder, Colo.: Westview Press, 1984, p. 49.

50. See David Ronfeldt: "Rethinking the Monroe Doctrine," in *Orbis* (April 1985).

51. Anthony Maingot: "The United States in the Caribbean: Geopolitics and the Bargaining Capacity of Small States," paper presented at the Colloquium on Peace, Development and Security in the Caribbean Basin: Perspectives to the Year 2000, Kingston, March 1987, p. 11.

52. Payne et al.: "Grenada," pp. 51–52.

53. See Lilia Bermudez: *Centroamérica y el conflicto de baja intensidad,* Mexico City: Siglo XXI, 1987.

54. See Robert Woodward: *Veil: The Secret Wars of the CIA 1981–1987,* London: Simon and Schuster, 1987.

55. Rodríguez Beruff: "Puerto Rico," pp. 71–81.

56. Ibid.

57. See Berkan et al.: "Las Violaciones."

58. See C. Sunshine: *The Caribbean: Survival, Struggle and Sovereignty,* Washington, D.C.: EPICA, 1985.

59. See Erisman: "Colossus Challenged."

60. See Greene: "The Ideological."

61. See Anthony Maingot: "Cuba and the Commonwealth Carribbean: Playing the Cuban Card," in *The New Cuban Presence,* edited by Barry Levine, Boulder, Colo.: Westview Press, 1983.

62. See Ronald E. Jones: "Cuba and the English-speaking Caribbean," in *Cuba in the World,* edited by Cole Blasier and Carmelo Mesa-Lago, Pittsburgh: Pittsburgh University Press, 1979.

63. Anthony Bryan: "Cuba's Impact in the Caribbean," in *International Journal,* 40 (1985), pp. 340–341.

64. Eric Williams: "The Foreign Relations of Trinidad and Tobago," address by the Honourable Dr. Eric Williams, on December 6, 1963, pp. 189–210.

65. See Fitzroy Ambursley: "Whither Grenada? An Investigation into the March 13th Revolution One Year After," in *Contemporary Caribbean: A Sociological Reader,* edited by Susan Craig, Maracas: The College Press, 1982.

66. See Edward González: "The Cuban and Soviet Challenge in the Caribbean Basin," in *Orbis* (Spring 1985).

67. See Jack Child: "Variables para la política de Estados Unidos en la Cuenca del Caribe en la década de 1980," in *Intereses occidentales y política de Estados Unidos en el Caribe,* edited by James R. Greene and Brent Scowcroft, Buenos Aires: Grupo Editor Latinoamericano, 1985.

68. See Dominguez: "Cuba's Relations."

69. Leslie Manigat: "Geopolítica de las relaciones entre Venezuela y el Caribe: problemática general y problemas," in *Geopolítica de las relaciones de Venezuela con el Caribe,* edited by Andres Serbin, Caracas: Fondo Editorial Acta Científica, 1983, p. 26.

70. Grenada was the only English-speaking Caribbean country that supported the Argentine position during the conflict, particularly in the OAS.

71. See Serbin: "Surinam."

72. Sutton: "Political Aspects," p. 35.

73. Laura Del Alizal: "Las relaciones de México con el Caribe," paper presented to the CLACSO International Relations Working Group, Puerto Rico, January 1988, p. 13.

74. Dora Rothlisberger: "Relaciones de Colombia con el Caribe insular," paper presented at the CLACSO International Relations Working Group, Puerto Rico, January, 1988, p. 28.

75. See Anthony Bryan: "The Commonwealth Caribbean/Latin American Relationship: New Wine in Old Bottles?" in *Caribbean Affairs,* 1, 1 (1988).

3
Toward Caribbean Militarization?

In 1986, two researchers from the English-speaking Caribbean compiled studies on militarization in the non-Hispanic Caribbean by various scholars in the region who were concerned with the effects of arms escalation and development of the armed forces in Caribbean societies.[1] In their introduction to this work, Young and Phillips defined the concept of militarization as follows:

> Militarization, whether in the Caribbean or in other parts of the Third World, refers to the tendency of a national military apparatus (armed forces, paramilitary organizations, intelligence and bureaucratic agencies) to assume increasing visibility, involvement, and control over the social lives and behavior of the citizenry. The process of militarization also encompasses military domination of national priorities and objectives at the expense of civilian institutions.[2]

This definition, applied to an analysis of Caribbean societies, agrees with the conclusions of some of the writers who contributed to the work that a militarization process indeed occurred in the non-Hispanic Caribbean during the 1980s and that this process has affected societies in the region. This position is also taken by several authors who do not hesitate to point out that the active military involvement of the United States in the region has affected Caribbean societies and led them to militarization.[3] Such an analysis, however, is questioned by other researchers who point out that only Cuba, and in the non-Hispanic Caribbean only Guyana and Grenada during the Bishop government, have actually undergone significant militarization as described by Young and Phillips.[4] This debate, whoever the participants may be, is not merely an academic exercise in semantics, since it sheds light on the problems relating to security and stability that face the Caribbean states, while simultaneously suggesting possibilities for effectively establishing a peace zone in the region.

First and foremost, it should be borne in mind that most of these studies originated in the English-speaking Caribbean and are not derived from a global understanding of the region. In line with the geopolitical picture described in preceding chapters, it should therefore be noted that an appropriate response to the question of whether a militarization process currently taking place in the Caribbean can only be based on an analysis of its global geopolitical dynamics.

However, given the limited scope of this work, only certain factors that tie the Caribbean to Central America will be touched on; attention will be focused on the island Caribbean and states linked to it, with a view to demonstrating that, despite current criteria, the latter do possess unique political, economic, and ethnohistorical characteristics that nonetheless do not necessarily dissociate them from global geopolitical dynamics.

Following the same general scheme as in the previous chapter, the degree of militarization to which the Caribbean states have been subjected will be analyzed; occasional recapitulation of elements already addressed will also be included in order to offer a more thorough study.

Militarization in the More Developed English-Speaking Caribbean States and Suriname

Consideration will first be given to the more developed CARICOM states. In the cases of Jamaica and Trinidad, the origin of their present military structures can be found in the New West Indies Regiment, created during the existence of the West Indies Federation, of which Batallions I and III became the Jamaica Regiment and Batallion II became the Trinidad and Tobago Regiment in 1962.[5] With the exception of Guyana and Belize, whose border disputes with Latin American neighbors caused an increased presence of British forces, these are the only military structures that came into existence in the English-speaking Caribbean during the decolonization process, as an offshoot of the British forces formerly present.

Despite the professionalism imposed upon these regiments during British rule, after independence military plots against the constitutional government were revealed on two occasions in Jamaica. As for Trinidad, during the February Revolution of 1970, members of the army carried out an uprising led, among others, by Lieutenant Rafique Shah, during which Prime Minister Eric Williams was forced to seek the military support of the United States and Venezuela.[6]

In 1981, during the elections that brought the present prime minister, Edward Seaga, to power, political violence with the participation of gangs and parapolice forces caused over 600 deaths in Jamaica.

As mentioned previously, the Seaga victory opened up the possibility for President Reagan's administration to turn Jamaica into a model of capitalist development in the region. However, in the process the country was also converted into a mainstay of the regional security policy developed by the White House. In 1981, the Seaga government was offered $1.5 million in military assistance.[7] Subsequently, Jamaica's military participation in the Grenada invasion allowed it to receive additional assistance in the amount of $4.2 million in 1983/84.[8]

Nevertheless, in the mid-1980s the military budgets of both Jamaica and Trinidad tended to decrease rather than rise. In Jamaica, an estimated budget of J $90 million in 1983/84 increased to J $112.3 million in 1984/85; however, exchange fluctuations caused the U.S. dollar value of the budget to fall from $38,880,000 to $25,560,000. In Trinidad, the reduction in military expenditure was even more marked, inasmuch as the 1984 budget of TT $195 million fell to TT $180 million in 1985, with a real fall from US $81,250,000 to US $73,470,000.[9]

The total amount of military troops in each country is also notably limited. In Jamaica, total troops in the Jamaican Defence Force (JDF) are 2,520 out of a population of 2,380,000. Of these troops, 150 are assigned to the coast guard and 170 to the air force.[10] However, an unconfirmed estimate of 6,000 men serve in the police forces, which have occasionally been involved in activities of the ruling Jamaica Labour Party.[11]

In Trinidad, of a total population of 1,209,000, there are 2,075 troops in the armed forces, with a full quarter of this number serving in the coast guard. Another 4,000 men are in the police forces.[12]

This situation strikes a sharp contrast with military development in Guyana, where, since 1964, the military structure has grown markedly and paramilitary and parapolice organizations have multiplied as well. Antecedents to this process can be found in the 1953 British military intervention following the electoral victory and rise to power of a Marxist-leaning government under the People's Progressive Party (PPP), which was representative of a nationalist movement with a broad popular base of multiethnic composition. Subsequent splintering of the PPP along ethnic lines did not keep the party from obtaining new electoral victories in 1957 and 1961.[13] Between 1962 and 1964, a destabilization campaign was launched against the Cheddi Jagan government and supported by the U.S. government, causing riots and ethnic polarization that threatened to lead British Guiana to civil war. This crisis marked the first U.S. intervention in the English-speaking Caribbean,[14] characterized by CIA involvement in the mobilization of unions and opposition parties to destabilize the Jagan government. This was implemented as part of the "no second Cuba policy" advocated by the United States at the time.[15]

With the support of Great Britain and the United States, Forbes Burnham and his People's National Congress (PNC) took over the government in 1964 and two years later led the country to political independence. The Guyana Defence Force was thus formed in 1965, with an initial force of 2,135 troops, organized and trained by British officers, and with a ratio of one member of the military for every 300 citizens. This changed, however, with an increase in the military and paramilitary structure to 17,708 between 1965 and 1984, yielding a new ratio of one member of the military for every 43 inhabitants.[16] Some of these troops are serving in the GDF, but three new paramilitary structures have been created since 1973: the Guyana National Service, formed in 1973 and aimed at recruiting young men for the defense and development of Guyanese society; the Guyana People's Militia, formed in 1976 as a GDF reserve force; and the National Guard Service, formed in 1980 to protect government offices and state property against possible sabotage by opposition groups.[17] In the late 1980s these paramilitary groups accounted for 1,500, 2,000, and 2,000 troops, respectively.

To this process of paramilitary development should be added the growth, during the 1970s, of parapolice groups such as the House of Israel, led by Rabbi Washington, who carried out acts of repression against dissidents and groups who opposed the PNC regime.

Accelerated military development in Guyana seemed justified in the light of a possible threat from Venezuela or, to a lesser extent, Suriname—both of which countries had ongoing border disputes with Guyana—or from the existence of a powerful neighbor, Brazil. Nevertheless, the main purpose was undoubtedly to control and repress any form of internal opposition and to provide a safety valve for absorbing a large unemployed sector of mostly Afro-Guyanese youths. Venezuelan military capacity, with an estimated 69,000 troops including the national guard,[18] and with modern military equipment that includes eleven Mirage aircraft and twenty-four F-16s in the air force,[19] can hardly be resisted by Guyanese defense capability, which does not even possess an air force.[20]

Paradoxically, Belize, another former British colony on the mainland, which is also threatened by a border conflict with a Latin American neighbor, has not embarked on such a militarization process.

Ever since its political independence was attained, Great Britain has maintained a contingent of 1,800 troops in Belize, at an annual cost of US $50 million. These troops are responsibile for training the 700 men belonging to the Belize Defence Force, which was created in 1978.[21] Great Britain has given no date for the withdrawal of its troops from Belize. Under these circumstances, U.S. military aid has substantially increased since 1982, when it provided US $26,000 for military training. By 1986, the figure for assistance for security programs in Belize had risen to US $5,100,000.[22] In addition to such financial assistance, the United States is sending military advisers to train the members of the BDF and, through the Military Education Training Program (IMET), military personnel from Belize have gone to the United States for training at U.S. bases.[23] The growing U.S. presence in Belize derives both from its geographical proximity to the critical Central American focus of conflicts and from the development in Belize of extensive drug production and marketing operations.

In Suriname, the establishment of a military government under Bouterse led to significant military development. This process, however, cannot be said to have militarized civilian society, despite the emergence and spread of Brunsjwik's "maroon" guerrillas in the eastern part of the country between 1986 and 1987. The Surinamese army was created in 1975, under the supervision of a Dutch military mission, with 350 troops and an initial budget of US $7.5 million. After independence, the civilian government attempted to form a coast guard and air force, while the army grew to 600 active troops with a budget of US $12 million for 1979.[24] After the military coup, troops were increased to 2,000 and the budget was raised to US $43 million in 1983; moreover, an attempt was made, beginning in 1982, to form a militia.[25] In 1988, troops serving in the army, marines, and air force amounted to 2,690, of which 240 belonged to the latter two forces.[26] The nation's militia as of that date numbered 900 men.[27]

From 1981 to 1983, a considerable portion of the military and the national militia were trained by Cuban military advisers who had arrived accompanied by technicians, medical doctors, and educators. After the Cubans were expelled in October 1983, military training and advisory were taken over mainly by Brazil.[28] Bouterse's rapprochement with Libya as of 1984 did not yield the expected results in the way of military assistance; instead, it provoked a reaction from France via neighboring French Guiana.

Expansion of the armed forces in a society with a population of less than 400,000 should be understood in the context of internal factors threatening the Bouterse regime. In the first place, it should be borne in mind that between 1980 and 1987, there were five coup attempts by factions of varying ideologies, all of which had army support or participation. Another factor contributing to this development was the emergence in 1986 of a guerrilla movement, based in the "maroon" areas and supported by political exiles living in Holland who enjoyed the tacit backing of France.

Notwithstanding all of the above, Surinamese society did not undergo notorious militarization; in the late 1980s a reversal of the political conditions imposed by the military regime was achieved and the parliamentary system reinstated, under a new constitution approved by referendum.

Militarization in Grenada During the Revolutionary Government

The militarization process of Guyana is comparable only to that of Grenada between 1979 and 1983. When the New Jewel Movement (NJM) took power on 13 March 1979, it carried out a surprise attack that neutralized the island's limited armed forces. The attack was the work of forty-five members of the NJM, led by Hudson Austin, an ex-corporal in the Grenadan army. Once the revolutionary government established itself, this group became the People's Revolutionary Army (PRA) and Austin was promoted to general.[29] Existing police forces were controlled by the new government and relegated to secondary duties (such as controlling traffic in the capital city of St. George's). When the United States invaded Grenada in 1983, the former 550 policemen had been reduced to only 180.[30]

The situation developed differently for the PRA, which rapidly grew to 600 troops out of a population of 110,000,[31] and plans were made to increase the army to 11,000 by 1986.[32] Between 1979 and 1983, the revolutionary government signed five military agreements with Cuba, the USSR, and North Korea, agreements that, among other things, helped to obtain weapons for the PRA. The bulk of Cuban economic assistance was concentrated in the airport project at Point Salines; the USSR also provided financial assistance amounting to US $25.8 million. Cuba sent twenty-seven permanent and twelve temporary military advisers and set up a military training program together with the Soviet Union.[33]

The various forms of popular organization promoted by the NJM during this period led to the creation of a popular militia, following the Cuban model. The ostensible purpose of this militarization process in Grenadan society was to guarantee an effective defense against a U.S. invasion, but this project was proved totally impracticable in October 1983, when the most effective source of resistance against U.S. troops turned out to be the Cuban construction workers, many of whom had had previous military training and experience.[34] The internal crisis of the NJM prior to the invasion was the result of increasing influence, in the party's central committee, of PRA officers who favored Bernard Coard's position. When the crisis broke out, Bishop was set free by a large number of his followers, who then moved to Fort Ruppert, where Bishop was assassinated on 18 October, together with other NJM leaders who supported him, by PRA troops who regained control of the fort. On 19 October, General Hudson Austin announced the dissolution of the revolutionary government and the creation of a revolutionary military council to replace it,[35] thus closing this chapter of the Grenadan revolutionary experiment, which was definitively ended by the military invasion that followed.

The Eastern Caribbean Microstates

Grenada's militarization process directly affected its English-speaking neighbors in the Eastern Caribbean. Many of them had already faced situations at some point since the beginning of their independence processes that internally or externally threatened their political stability.

In St. Vincent in December 1979, Prime Minister Milton Cato was faced two days after his re-election with an uprising by a group of Rastafarians on Union Island in the Grenadines chain. The uprising was led by Lennox "Bumper" Charles, who demanded increased attention by the St. Vincent government to the problems of his small island. The Rastafarians took over the airport and the police station, forcing the government to send a police contingent to repress the uprising. "Bumper" Charles fled to Grenada, but was returned by PRG authorities to St. Vincent, where he was tried and sent to prison. During the crisis, the Cato government requested and obtained the support of the government of Barbados.[36] However, tensions between the Grenadines and the central government in St. Vincent abated only with the election to office of Grenadines native James Mitchell.

Dominica was almost sold in 1974 to a Texan "ghost" company that represented South African interests; a similar situation arose again in 1980.[37] In 1981, as mentioned, Prime Minister Eugenia Charles was forced to deal with three attempts to overthrow her government, two of them promoted by former Prime Minister Patrick John with the participation of members of the Dominica Defence Force (DDF) (afterward disbanded) and the third by a group of mercenaries serving the Mafia and the Ku Klux Klan. These coup attempts were suppressed with the aid of intelligence provided by the FBI and French military assistance received from Guadeloupe and Martinique.[38]

In St. Lucia, the internal crisis and the split in the ruling St. Lucia Labour Party (SLLP) in 1982 culminated in a situation of instability. In August of the following year, the new government of Prime Minister Compton denounced Libyan training of local terrorists to destabilize the island, pointing to an SLLP leader as the promoting agent.[39]

A secessionist movement has existed in Barbuda since before the independence of Antigua and Barbuda, an island of approximately 1,500 inhabitants. The government of Prime Minister Vere Bird has been repeatedly accused of links with syndicated crime and drug trafficking, to the extent that in 1979, a scandal broke out in relation to the establishment on Antigua of the Space Research Corporation, involving arms trafficking to South Africa. A similar situation arose during the St. Kitts-Nevis decolonization process, when, in 1967, Anguilla—a third island and an administrative dependent of St. Kitts—rebelled against the capital and provoked the intervention of British troops; in the end, Anguilla remained an associated British state. This has not kept tension from persisting between the other two islands, which are integrated into one single independent state.

Even Barbados has not been free of such situations. In November 1976, a plot was uncovered wherein two individuals, Banks and Burnett-Alleyne, were planning to overthrow the Barbados Labour Party (BLP) government. Burnett-Alleyne, who had prior links with the Barbados Democratic Party, tried once again to overthrow the BLP government in December 1978 by invading with a group of mercenaries sent over from Dominica. The invasion was backed by the former prime minister of Dominica, Patrick John, and was intended to convert Barbados into an operations base for arms traffickers linked to South Africa.[40] The attempt was again thwarted, thanks to intelligence received from the United States and France.[41] As a result, however, a drastic shift took place in the government's defense policy and expansion of the Barbados Defence Force was encouraged.[42]

Drug Trafficking in the Caribbean

In addition to this general picture, the Bahamas have repeatedly been denounced for laundering drug money at offshore banking facilities. In 1985, members of Prime Minister Sir Lynden Pendling's government were accused of involvement in drug trafficking to the United States. The lack of control over the numerous keys in the archipelago makes them convenient trans-shipment points for South American drugs en route to the United States.[43] Some British colonial dependencies have also been involved in this process. In March 1986, Turks and Caicos authorities were arrested for smuggling drugs into the United States; all members of government in these islands were removed from their posts in July 1986, after British intervention.[44]

The new government of Trinidad and Tobago also faced a major scandal, which revealed the involvement of high-ranking police officers, magistrates, and politicians in drug trafficking.[45] This scandal unleashed a long chain of accusations; crime syndicates were found to be dealing in arms traffic and in prostitution of immigrants arriving from Colombia, Haiti, Venezuela, and the Dominican Republic,[46] activities that also involved former government officials.

However, the English-speaking states most directly linked to the production of drugs are probably Jamaica and Belize, the principal marijuana producers in the area. Jamaican production of marijuana for export stood at 1,485 to 2,025 tons in 1986, with production in Belize at some 550 tons for the same year.[47] A former minister of Belize was arrested in Miami in April 1985 for supplying 5,000 pounds of marijuana monthly to distribution centers in the United States.[48] Growth in Jamaican marijuana production has been such that unofficial estimates point to marijuana as the country's third-largest export product. The participation of Jamaican immigrants in the United States in drug trafficking has turned the so-called Jamaican "posses" into some of the most powerful criminal organizations in the country.[49]

Aside from the production of marijuana in Jamaica and Belize, however, the principal drug problem in the region lies in the fact that certain islands have become key points for the traffic in cocaine and heroin from Latin American drug-producing countries. Drug trafficking is expedited not only by offshore banking facilities in islands such as the Bahamas, but also by the corruption of Caribbean governments or individuals who facilitate smuggling from the region itself or from South American producers. This phenomenon is typical not only of the English-speaking Caribbean; in 1986, a military officer with close ties to the Bouterse government in Suriname was arrested in Miami and accused of smuggling drugs from Colombia. Bouterse's government has also been accused of supplying passports, visas, and banking services to Colombian drug traffickers.[50] Cuba and Haiti have likewise been accused of channeling drugs to the United States and Europe.[51] The case of Haiti has particular political repercussions, since a sector of the armed forces, among them the notorious Colonel Paul who led the Dessalines Regiment, is said to be involved in smuggling drugs into the United States. This situation generates specific obstacles to democratization in Haiti.[52] In the region generally, the development of drug trafficking has led to a far greater involvement there by U.S. government agencies and organizations working to control the problem. In fact, the Drug Enforcement Agency (DEA) has increased its activities both in the non-Hispanic Caribbean islands and in mainland territories. This process has, furthermore, deepened the region's security problems, thus affecting Caribbean societies and their stability. That is to say, the various U.S. police and intelligence agencies have been increasingly involved in the Caribbean, and military maneuvers aimed at controlling the drug problem, such as Operation Hat Trick opposite the Colombian coastline in 1984, have also increased. These developments were the result of a U.S. policy aimed at controlling drug production and trafficking, rather than repressing its demand and consumption in the United States.

Regional Defense Agreements and Stability in the Eastern Caribbean Before and After the Grenada Crisis

Discussion of the need to create a regional armed force began among the Eastern Caribbean microstates long before the Grenadan revolutionary experience was perceived as a threat to stability, and before the actions of mercenaries, organized crime, or drug traffickers posed the real possibilities of destabilization and interruption of democratic regimes in the region. The first coup attempts against the governments of Dominica and Antigua, in 1967, and the secessionist rebellion in Anguilla during the same year, gave rise to the first regional talks on the advisability of establishing a regional defense force. No agreement was reached at the regional level at the time, owing mainly to the logistical incapacity of the microstates to provide for themselves without the cooperation of the more developed states.[53]

In July 1979, the first sounds of alarm were heard in reaction to the influence of the Grenadan revolution, after a meeting in St. George's that was attended by Louisy, George Odlum, and Josie of the SLLP, radical leaders Seraphine and Martin of Dominica, and Maurice Bishop. The meeting produced a final declaration by the NJM in support of the revolutionaries of neighboring islands and it revealed the effective threat that the Grenadan revolutionary process could pose to the stability of the island governments.

In October 1982, therefore, a memorandum of understanding was signed by the governments of Dominica, St. Lucia, Antigua, St. Vincent, and Barbados, for the purpose of mutual assistance and cooperation for security and defense.[54] The memorandum set out three objectives: (1) to coordinate security policies among the signatory states; (2) to prepare plans for the use of police and defense forces at a regional level; and (3) to create an operations command to direct these forces according to the requirements of the signatory states.[55] The agreement explicitly excluded Grenada, which was a member of the OECS, and included Barbados, which had never been a member. The Barbados government contributed toward the establishment and location of this command and covered 49 percent of budgeted expenses. It should be noted that Article 8 of the Defense and Security Committee of the OECS treaty was not invoked in this context, although, except for the inclusion of Grenada, its objectives were almost identical to those of the memorandum.[56]

The Memorandum of 1982 led to the creation of the Regional Security System (RSS), headquartered in Barbados and supported by the U.S. Embassy in that country.[57] At the same time, during the summit conference in November 1982 at Ocho Ríos, Jamaica, CARICOM began to discuss the possibility of signing a broader mutual assistance treaty. No decision was reached at the meeting, but a working group was formed to discuss the options. This working group defined three options, based on interests in the region: (1) to join the Río Treaty (TIAR); (2) to sign a similar treaty that would be restricted to the Caribbean states; and (3) to work toward the establishment of nonaggression pacts with potentially hostile nations. Option (1) was rejected first, because it opened up possibilities for U.S. intervention in the area and for U.S. support of Latin American countries engaged in border disputes with Caribbean nations. In general, the suggestions that prevailed were those that proposed a nonaggression pact between the United States and Cuba and the establishment of a peace zone in the region.[58] CARICOM accepted none of these suggestions, however, and in the end, nothing came of the proposals. Nevertheless, the fact that these proposals were made revealed the tensions existing within the organization at the time in regard to effective threats in the region.

Some CARICOM members held the opinion—and later sustained it by taking sides during the Grenada invasion—that the principles of political pluralism and nonintervention advocated within the context of regional solidarity should not be contested by the establishment of a defense and assistance treaty in the English-speaking Caribbean. This perspective also implied that any agreement of this type should necessarily exclude extraregional actors, such as the United States.

In contrast, for the United States, within the regional policy framework outlined by the Reagan administration, consolidation of Grenada's revolutionary experiment was an even greater threat than the operations of drug or arms traffickers, inasmuch as it contributed to consolidating the

Cuban influence in the region and further extended Soviet-Cuban expansionism, with obvious consequences for Central America.

As of the date when Maurice Bishop became prime minister, relations between the United States and the NJM government began to deteriorate. Shortly after the coup against Eric Gairy, Bishop requested the economic assistance of the United States and was offered $5,000. The rapid establishment of ties with Cuba and the Socialist bloc, as well as Grenada's support of the Soviet invasion of Afghanistan, did little to gain U.S. sympathy. In the process, which is analyzed elsewhere,[59] the United States tended to multiply its military exercises in the Caribbean and militarily reinforce its allies.[60] Puerto Rico served as a base for the military operations, while Jamaica and Barbados received the reinforcements. In this context, development of a regional security force became a top priority.

When the October crisis offered an opportunity for a U.S. invasion, 6,500 U.S. troops participated in it—together with limited contingents from Jamaica, Barbados, and the Eastern Caribbean states, as part of the regional "peace force" created on the basis of the Memorandum of 1982. Within this framework, one of the principal actors urging formation of a regional armed force was Prime Minister Tom Adams of Barbados. The "Adams Doctrine" called for the creation of a multinational regional security system, with the participation of 1,000 troops from seven Eastern Caribbean microstates, to be headquartered in Barbados and led by Brigadier General Rudyard Lewis, then commander of the BDF.[61]

Quite aside from the debate originated by this proposal, immediately after the invasion the United States began to create special forty-man units in each country—known as the Special Service Units (SSU)—which would work with the local police forces and receive training as of November 1983. These units were differentiated from the local armed forces (only Barbados and Antigua had regular armed forces) by their paramilitary capacity, and by their emphasis on drug control and repression of any future threats to the stability of the respective governments.

Police forces continued to be trained by Great Britain at their regional headquarters in Barbados.[62]

The creation of the SSU was not a sufficient response to Adams' initiative to create a regional security force. His proposal was supported by Prime Minister John Compton of St. Lucia, and at first enjoyed the backing of the Dominica government, which was especially involved in supporting U.S. intervention in Grenada. However, the victory of moderate James Mitchell in St. Vincent and of Errol Barrow in Barbados the following year changed the direction of events, since both expressed their disapproval of the initiative. Mitchell particularly demonstrated his position when he referred to the indiscriminate use of the SSU to stifle internal opposition in some of the Eastern Caribbean states.[63]

To Mitchell's and Barrow's reluctance was added the unwillingness of the United States and Great Britain to cover expenses for an undertaking that made no great contribution to their strategic objectives in the region, which, in principle, were guaranteed by their own forces.

Extraregional Actors, Arms Escalation, and Militarization in the Caribbean

It can be concluded that the arms escalation process experienced in the region basically has reflected global confrontation, and that one of the extraregional actors most deeply involved in the process is the United States. As mentioned previously, long-term U.S. objectives in the hemisphere have mainly embodied the desire of the United States to ensure its hegemony, consolidate the stability of regional states as a function of this hegemony, and prevent and exclude the influence of actors from outside the hemisphere.

These long-term goals, which were traditionally a part of U.S. policy toward Latin America, acquire specific features in the context of the Caribbean Basin and the geopolitical dynamics developed in the region since the 1970s. Jack Child defines U.S. policy in the region more closely, particularly as regards present circumstances. He points to three basic objectives: (1) establishment and maintenance of a secure, peaceful, stable, and friendly southern flank; (2) guaranteed access to raw materials, to trade and investment opportunities, and to sea routes through the region; and (3) exclusion of hostile powers from the area; all of which should be achieved at minimum cost and effort, within the context of the dynamics of the confrontation with the Soviet Union.[64]

The consolidation of a secure situation along its southern flank, which is also tied to increasing U.S. economic integration with the Caribbean Basin, has required the development of a policy aimed at neutralizing external threats, implementing détente with respect to possible intraregional tensions, and breaking down any internal conflicts that may arise among the states in the region.[65] From this perspective, the Caribbean Basin has been accorded top geopolitical, strategic, and military priority, and a line has been drawn to differentiate between the subregion and Central America—with the latter representing a direct threat to the attainment of these objectives and the Caribbean representing a potential threat, within the context of U.S. prioritization of the region as a function of its hemispheric hegemony.[66] The region has acquired fundamental strategic importance, both because of the objectives already described and because of the conviction, strongly upheld by the Reagan and Bush administrations, that for purposes of the global confrontation, it is vital to maintain an image of complete control over such an important area.[67]

Consequently, in the early 1980s, the U.S. military presence and the arms escalation among U.S. allies in the region grew considerably, in response to a predominantly geostrategic and military interpretation of the crisis and an identification of "Soviet expansionism" as its detonator.

The growth in U.S. military activity in the region has been channeled through increased maneuvers and an expansion of the Caribbean bases, as well as through training programs and military and police assistance programs, together with an increase in arms sales to the Caribbean states.

A Caribbean Joint Task Force in Key West, Florida, was established, which later became part of the U.S. Caribbean Command, one of three NATO commands.[68] Besides the military bases located in Panama, the United States has an extensive network of Caribbean facilities, principally in Puerto Rico. In addition to the Roosevelt Roads naval facilities of Sabana Seca and Vieques, there are two army and national guard training camps in Puerto Rico, along with a training camp and administrative center at Fort Buchanan. In 1983, the Ramey Air Base at Aguadilla[69] was reactivated. The Roosevelt Roads Naval Base is the center of the navy control system for the Caribbean and the South Atlantic, with an estimated annual mobilization of 45,000 aircraft and 1,200 ships.[70]

As shown in Table 3.1, there are also military bases at Antigua, the Bahamas, and Bermuda, each of which has specific operational and logistical

Table 3.1 U.S. Military Installations in the Caribbean

Location	*Personnel*	
Antigua	Navy	191
	Air Force	na
Bahamas	Navy	na
	Air Force	na
Bermuda	Navy	na
	Navy	1,904
	Navy	175
Cuba	Navy	2,673
Puerto Rico	Army, National Guard	122
	Army	1,053
	Navy	3,009
	Navy	459
	Navy	na
	Air Force, National Guard	994
	Total	10,580

Source: T. Barry, B. Wood, and D. Preusch: *The Other Side of Paradise* (New York: Grove Press, 1984) p. 199.

functions; there are, furthermore, the Guantanamo naval base in Cuba and the vital and strategic military installations in Panama. The latter include Fort Amador, the 193rd Infantry Brigade headquarters; Fort Gulick, headquarters of the School of the Americas; and the Southern Command general headquarters at Quarry Heights and Howard Air Base.

U.S. military exercises in the region have been stepped up since 1980. A previous exercise at Guantanamo, in Cuba in 1979, had set a precedent, but Operation Solid Shield in May 1980 was the first military exercise in the Caribbean. In subsequent years, these maneuvers continued without interruption

Table 3.2 U.S. Military Maneuvers in the Caribbean 1974–1984

1979	Guantanamo, 1,800 Marines
1980 Solid Shield	Guantanamo and Puerto Rico, 20,000 troops, 42 ships, and 350 aircraft
1980 Readex	Guantanamo and Puerto Rico
1981 Ocean Venture	16,870 troops, 12 ships, and 100 aircraft
1981 Falcon's Eye	Puerto Cortés, Honduras
1982 No Name	Joint exercises with Canada in Gulf of Mexico and Florida straits
1982 Readex	War games, 39 ships, 200 aircraft and one British ship, with amphibian assault practice on Vieques Island
1982 Ocean Venture	45,000 troops, 60 ships, 350 aircraft; lasted one month, with Dutch forces participating
1982 Falcon Vista	Navy exercises with Honduras
1982 Safepass	War games north of Cuba, with six Western countries participating (NATO)
1983 Kindle Liberty	Training in Panama for defense of canal, 3,000 U.S. troops and 7,000 Panamanian troops
1983 Readex	War games, 43 ships, including British and Dutch ships
1983 Universal Trek	Land and sea maneuvers, 5,000 U.S. troops and National Guard
1983 Unitas	Joint exercises between navy and Latin American countries carried out in Caribbean, 2,000 U.S. troops and 12,000 Latin American
1983 No Notice Exercise	Navy exercises after Grenada invasion, with 8 ships
1984 OceanVenture	Guantanamo, Florida straits, and Gulf of Mexico, 30,000 troops and 350 ships
1984 Unitas	Navy exercises in Caribbean and Latin America with U.S. ships
1984 Composite	Navy exercises in the Atlantic Ocean and Caribbean Sea, near Puerto Training Unit 1-85 Rico, with 25 U.S. ships
1984 No Name	Eastern Caribbean, with U.S. destroyer and Eastern Caribbean states coast guards

Sources: "Proyecto Caribeño de Justicia y Paz," Puerto Rico, June–July 1982, and R. Escobar, "Cronología de las Maniobras Militares Norteamericanas en América Latina," in *Cuadernos de Nuestra América* 2, no. 4 (1985).

Note: Only exercises in the West Indies and Panama have been taken into consideration.

Table 3.3 U.S. Armed Forces and Military Assistance in the Caribbean

	Regular Armed Forces 1986–1987	*U.S.-Trained Personnel 1980–1983*	*U.S. Military Assistance 1981–1984*[a]
Bahamas	497	na	5
Belize	600	na	na
Eastern Caribbean [b]	250[c]	128	10,810
Cuba	162,000	0	0
Guyana	5,450	50	98
Haiti	8,000[d]	95	1,125
Jamaica	2,100	101	7,797
Dominican Republic	21,300	496	15,607
Suriname	2,535	14	53
Trinidad and Tobago	2,130	na	15

Source: Paul Sutton: "The Caribbean as a Focus for Strategic and Resource Rivalry," in *Central American Security System,* ed. P. Calvert (New York: Cambridge University Press, 1988).
Notes: [a]Figures are in U.S. $ millions. Includes Foreign Military Sales (FMS), Military Assistance Program (MAP), and International Military Educational Training (IMET).
[b]Includes Antigua, Barbados, Dominica, St. Lucia, and St. Vincent.
[c]Figures for 1980.
[d]Figures for 1982.

until the Grenada invasion in October 1983.[71] Some of the exercises also involved British and Dutch forces, as shown in Table 3.2.

In addition to the expansion of military bases and implementation of Caribbean maneuvers, training programs and military assistance to the region also increased as of 1980. The training of Haitian and Dominican Republic troops carried out in earlier years was now expanded to include Antigua, Barbados, Dominica, Jamaica, St. Lucia, St. Vincent, Guyana, and Suriname.[72] Moreover, military assistance to the Caribbean, including IMET programs, increased sevenfold[73] between 1979 and 1983.

The process of increasing U.S. military assistance and involvement in the region reached a climax with the dramatic military deployment carried out during the Grenada invasion, when eleven ships, including the USS *Independence* with ninety combat aircraft on board, served as backup for 1,800 invading marines from the 22nd Amphibian Unit, two army batallions with 600 troops each, and 3,000 men from the 82nd Airborne Division.[74]

The Grenada invasion marked the high point in the process of increasing U.S. military involvement in the Caribbean, in an effort to neutralize and eliminate any Cuban-Soviet influence and stabilize the area. The process also reflects increasing Soviet involvement in the region and dramatic military development in Cuba, where Soviet naval strength increased considerably in the late 1980s along with growth of the Cuban armed forces.

The Soviet presence in the region has been a source of repeated tensions with the United States, and spurred the signing of three agreements in relation to Soviet forces stationed in Cuba. The first of these agreements, signed in 1962 after the "missile crisis," stipulated that, in exchange for U.S. assurance of nonintervention in Cuba, the Soviet Union would not place strategic arms on the island. In 1970, a second agreement committed the USSR to refrain from the use of Cuban ports as strategic operations bases, particularly in view of the existence of Soviet submarines in the area. Finally, in 1979, after a Soviet brigade was detected on the island, it was agreed that the Soviet Union would not keep combat troops on Cuban territory and that Soviet military personnel would be limited to advisers and technicians.[75]

However, increasing Soviet naval strength was ensured, as of 1969, by the arrival in the Caribbean of twenty-three Soviet fleets of small vessels, supplied in and operating from Cuban ports, particularly the Cienfuegos base.[76] Consequently, expansion of Soviet naval power worldwide not only posed a threat to the United States along the Pacific Coast, but also succeeded in building up a significant presence in the U.S. southeastern flank. Moreover, the Soviet Union provided Cuba with the largest navy in the Caribbean. As of 1981, as part of the Soviet arms programs,[77] Cuba had acquired two Koni frigates and other substantial naval supplies, including three submarines.[78]

Soviet TU-950 Bear reconnaissance aircraft use the San Antonio de los Baños and José Martí air bases regularly and two antisubmarine TU-144 F aircraft[79] have been on the island since March 1983. By the same token, with Soviet assistance, Cuba has built up one of the best-equipped air forces in Latin America, whose pilots have gained combat experience in Africa. In addition to the considerable defensive capacity of this force, estimated in 1984 at 270 MIGs, with adequate support bases in the region, the Cuban air force could bring its strength to bear not only on the southeastern United States but also on some of the mainland South American countries.

Soviet troops stationed in Cuba are of limited offensive capacity. This force is composed principally of a brigade of 2,600 to 3,000 troops, a group of 2,500 advisers, and an electronic monitoring base at Lourdes, which is thought to be the largest of its type outside the Soviet Union.[80] In contrast, the Cuban armed forces have increased from 109,000 in 1970 to 190,000 in 1987, not including reserve, militia, and paramilitary forces.[81]

The above facts reveal that, aside from the freedom of circulation enjoyed by the Soviet navy, the military presence of the USSR is relatively restricted in the Caribbean. From a strictly military point of view, both the Soviet presence and the accelerated military development of Cuba pose a limited threat to the United States and to the sea-lanes crossing the region. As pointed out by a U.S. military analyst, "Cuban ports and airbases could not long survive a U.S. counterattack launched from Navy facilities in the southern states. Even in a worst-case scenario with a concerted Soviet-Cuban interdiction campaign in the Caribbean, Secretary of the Navy John Lehman believes the Navy could 'fight through'."[82]

In this regard, the increased U.S. presence in the area is not simply a response to a possible Cuban and Soviet military threat to its southeastern flank. Political stability in the region is also a principal concern of the United States, a concern that was directly tied, from the point of view of the Reagan administration, to the degree of influence exercised by Cuba and the Soviet Union in the Caribbean. A substantial portion of the arms buildup and military training and assistance to the states in the region has therefore been linked to counterinsurgency objectives, aimed both at neutralizing the influence of revolutionary processes, as in the case of Grenada, and at controlling and repressing radical elements in the Caribbean. These objectives underlie the ongoing emphasis on the training of police and intelligence forces and initiatives designed to establish a regional security system.

However, in light of U.S. policy objectives toward the Caribbean and with respect to economic, political, and military costs vis-à-vis the global conflict, it would seem more advisable for the United States to maintain its own military presence in the region and to reinforce police and intelligence services, rather than to finance a buildup of armed forces that might eventually result in politically unstable situations. The complexity of the issues is compounded, moreover, by regional security concerns in regard to uncontrolled migration to the United States, terrorism, and the increase in drug trafficking. As illustrated by the situations unleashed in Haiti, the Bahamas, and Trinidad, to name only a few, the United States would do well not to rely totally on local efforts to control production and marketing of drugs in the region.

Political stability in the open and highly vulnerable societies of the Caribbean does not rest on military controls alone, which are structured on the basis of strategic and geopolitical concerns. The social and economic situation of the Caribbean populations, which are experiencing growing unemployment and poverty and the severe consequences of the financial crisis, constitutes a detonating factor with respect to increasing political and social tensions. For this reason, the former colonial metropolitan centers of Britain, France, and the Netherlands have preferred to maximize the effect of their regional efforts through economic assistance programs, although this does not stand in the way of their contributing to the reinforcement of police forces and, especially, intelligence agencies.

Great Britain keeps limited contingents in the Caribbean, stationed mainly in Belize, and carries out military and police assistance programs, which have grown significantly, particularly since the Grenadan crisis. In addition to maintaining stability in the region, in line with U.S. and Western interests, one of its main strategic concerns is also to guarantee the availability of operational bases for action in the South Atlantic. In turn, both Great Britain and the Netherlands, and more recently, France, have emphasized their presence in the area by means of joint exercises with the United States. France, however, is attempting to maintain a separate identity, through its garrisons in the DOM and by adhering to its own strategic interests in the region. These are linked to the Kourou aerospace base, the need for access to the French Pacific territories, and naval expansion at the world level. Canada's projects in the region are basically assistance programs; it has no military involvement. However, when the possibility of a security system was discussed for the Eastern Caribbean, Canada considered contributing part of the necessary funding for its maintenance.

The Latin American countries involved in the region have for the most part promoted economic assistance and cooperation programs with the Caribbean states in order to guarantee regional stability. This policy has been particularly evident in the cases of Mexico, Colombia, and Venezuela. Border tensions between the latter two countries, however, and between Venezuela and Guyana, have been a factor in military development; and the effects of the East-West confrontation as well as the security concerns of Colombia and Venezuela have occasionally reinforced their regional competition with Cuba. The development of their respective military capabilities has nonetheless had little impact on Caribbean militarization, with the exception of the accelerated militarization in Guyana in response to its conflict with Venezuela. Another Latin American actor who has contributed to the regional militarization process is Brazil, through its military advisory and assistance programs for Guyana and Suriname.

In summary, militarization and growth of the armed forces in the Caribbean during the 1980s were primarily the result of the strategic interests of the great powers and their impact on the region. On the conventional scale, the arms buildup owed only little to intraregional conflicts and tensions. Both the militarization of Cuba and Grenada and the attempts to establish a regional security system in the Eastern Caribbean—as well as the building up of the armed forces in Haiti and the Dominican Republic—should be seen in this light.

Once the Grenada intervention had taken place, the United States and various regional actors chose to substantially reduce regional military development. In this regard, political changes in the Eastern Caribbean have led to reconsideration of the need for a regional security force. The economic difficulties faced by Jamaica and Trinidad, as well as the process of democratization initiated in Suriname, have also given rise to a reduction in their military expenditures.

In fact, the reduction in the Cuban military presence in the area has caused the United States progressively to redefine its own military presence,[83] while altering as well its perception of regional actors in relation to regional security. The willingness by several regional actors to reverse the arms buildup and limit their military presence in the region has converged with the oft-repeated appeal for converting the Caribbean into a peace zone. Nonetheless, the vulnerability of the Caribbean states vis-à-vis internal and external threats, and regional differences that have prevented the achievement of various forms of economic and political integration, are clearly obstacles to the viability of such an initiative, in a region, furthermore, that is particularly sensitive to the effects of global confrontation.

Viability and Vulnerability of the Microstates

"Small is dangerous, small is vulnerable."[84]

The internal crisis unleashed in Grenada in October 1983 and its regional consequences, together with the South Atlantic crisis that began with the invasion of the Malvinas (Falklands) islands by Argentine armed forces in April 1982, has brought to the fore the vulnerability of microstates and the effects that their political instability may have on the world system. In particular, the Grenadan crisis has highlighted the importance of both internal processes and external pressures in small states, as well as their capacity to face these situations without endangering their own stability, that of the region, or in the long run, the international system as a whole.

The topic of the viability of small states, which was raised during the decolonization processes in the postwar period, had significant repercussions between 1955 and 1960 within the United Nations, when these decolonization processes accelerated. As mentioned by Martínez Sotomayor at the time, the problem of "viability" referred to the

> concern for the fact that a territory is too small in geographical size or otherwise, when the lands are insufficient or poor in natural or agricultural resources; which is sparsely settled by people whose leaders lack a minimum amount of training; and whose forms of government or administration are so precarious that the possibility of their developing as a sovereign nation and independent state would be an illusion.[85]

This concern led to a prolonged debate on the capacity of small territories, particularly the small island states in the Caribbean and the Pacific, to assume full sovereignty. Within the framework of the United Nations, while Afro-Asian states insisted on the need to proceed to absolute independence despite these observations, a number of the Latin American states proposed intermediate measures—such as free association or integration to a larger independent state—as a means for obtaining greater autonomy without jeopardizing their effective sovereignty. [86]The final decision in the United Nations to recognize the juridical equality of states regardless of their size, which was the principle that finally prevailed, was initially questioned by both the United States and Great Britain. The United States proposed that microstates should join the United Nations as associate members, paying a nominal quota. A similar proposal was made by the United Kingdom, with the suggestion that the nominal quota be eliminated.[87] Other proposals included the possibility of considering their accession to the organization as observers.

As a whole, these proposals reflected the concern that microstates, if accepted on equal terms, might acquire political significance out of proportion to their actual role in the international system.[88]

Since no microstate was willing to accept being a "second-class citizen," none of these proposals was accepted. Most microstates joined the international organization with full rights. There were, however, two notable exceptions: the Maldivas islands and St. Vincent and the Grenadines, which chose "special member" status at the time and which requested recognition as full members of the United Nations only in the 1980s.[89]

After the impasse produced in the 1960s by this debate, for over twenty years the principle that in juridical terms, all sovereign states are equal in the international system regardless of their size and population,[90] seemed to prevail as uncontested doctrine. In the early 1980s, however, the problem of the viability of microstates arose once again, particularly as a result of the international crisis caused by the Malvinas conflict and the Grenada invasion. This time the problem centered on the vulnerability of small nations. The security of microstates becomes a problem with broad consequences when crises occur that affect not only the society in question but also the region; in the long run, events of this order may cause a major international crisis. In this context, the United Kingdom and the Commonwealth took a special interest in the problem, having found that, if a population of under 1 million were said to define a microstate, of 49 Commonwealth members, 27 fell in this category. If the same criterion were imposed, 12 of the independent Caribbean states plus Suriname[91] would fall in this category; and owing to their vulnerability, special problems would arise with respect to national, regional, and international security. A UN study went even further, stating that all Commonwealth countries in the Caribbean should be considered microstates because of their geographical size, population, and GNP.[92]

The vulnerability of the Caribbean microstates is generally understood in relation to threats to their security.[93] These threats are classified into three categories: (1) threats to territorial security; (2) threats to political security; and (3) threats to economic security.[94] If we adhere to this general classification, we find that the non-Hispanic Caribbean states are frequently vulnerable according to all three classifications.

In regard to threats to territorial security, military threats such as direct aggression or invasion can be identified in the cases of Guyana, Belize, and

Grenada; and the establishment of foreign bases in the region and secession of smaller islands have also occurred. Nonmilitary threats linked to nongovernmental or private activities, such as arms or drug trafficking, often endanger the security of these states as well, especially in the Eastern Caribbean. In some cases, moreover, the demarcation of the respective exclusive economic zones has caused problems that also threaten territorial security. Yet, with the exception of the Grenada invasion, none of these threats has seriously jeopardized the security of the non-Hispanic Caribbean states. Serious tension produced by latent border conflicts, however, has at times resulted in the involvement of outside forces, as has also been the case in internal crises arising from arms smuggling, drug trafficking, or other criminal activities.

Political security threats have been more devastating than the threats of the first category. Ranging from the action of larger states exercising economic pressure over such countries as Jamaica, Grenada, Guyana, and Suriname, to adverse media campaigns and attempts against extraterritorial jurisdiction, the non-Hispanic Caribbean has experienced various forms of destabilization, generally undertaken to further U.S. interests. To these measures must be added the threats to political security arising from internal factors that relate indirectly to external interests, as in the case of subversive activity. For example, there have been guerrilla outbursts and terrorist activity among the pro-independence groups in the French DOMS (and in Puerto Rico) as well as in guerrilla focal points in Jamaica in the 1960s, in Trinidad in the 1970s, and in Suriname in the 1980s. A Rastafarian guerrilla group in Jamaica emerged as a result of internal political and economic factors; other groups, however, have been prompted by a combination of internal factors and external interests, as in the case of the "maroon" guerrillas in Suriname or the terrorist groups trained by Libya.

Nevertheless, particularly in the English-speaking Caribbean, neither limited geographical and demographical size nor financial obstacles to implementing political/military and intelligence security mechanisms is related to the weakness of the political systems. As pointed out by Paul Sutton,[95] a certain degree of stability has prevailed. This can be attributed principally to the high level of institutional loyalty toward the political model inherited from the metropolitan center, the pervasive government influence in civilian life, and the political harmony achieved within a framework of conservative pragmatism that generally leads parties in power to adhere to the political center so as to prevent effective dissent. To these stabilizing characteristics of the Caribbean microstates may be added "a foreign policy which reacts and is passive, seeking support in international law and in the functioning of international organizations in order to safeguard their security for the long term."[96]

However, as mentioned in the Grenadan case, recourse to international law and the support of regional or international organizations have not always been effective, mainly because of the incapacity of these organizations to halt the consequences of the East-West confrontation.[97]

Finally, threats to the economic security of the microstates arise as well because of their small size, their lack of natural and human resources, their dependence on external markets, and the predominant influence of economically powerful countries that find the relative openness of their basic economies useful. Their narrow economic structures make them particularly vulnerable to the impact of internal and external economic shocks, and to the socioeconomic and political aftermath of such crises. Moreover, the inadequacy of mechanisms for multilateral cooperation makes them more vulnerable to external control and influence, while economic cooperation arrangements with larger countries (generally conceived in bilateral terms) may represent risks for their long-term economic independence, as shown by the increase in external indebtedness of many non-Hispanic Caribbean countries. The economic advantages offered by the establishment of foreign bases or by investments by foreign companies or corporations may, likewise, represent risks to the economic security of these states.[98]

Economic threats in general are found to be related to political threats, especially in the context of East-West confrontation; moreover, development strategies may even reinforce the economic dependence of the microstates. The political and social costs of some economic programs implemented in the region are evidence of this.

Therefore, in the general context of security threats faced by the non-Hispanic Caribbean countries, the effects of the global polarization between the Western and socialist blocs and the impact of their confrontation in the region have been highly significant in political and economic terms, as well as in military terms. Indeed, the crisis that has had the greatest impact in the region in the last twenty-five years, with international reverberations as well, was the Grenadan crisis, a product of this confrontation. After the Grenada invasion, however, the massive arms buildup and militarization processes have not caused an increase in the emergence of new critical focal points in the region.

It is in this framework that a new shift has occurred in U.S. foreign policy. Now that a temporary stabilization has been achieved in the region, the United States has tended to abandon its interest in the non-Hispanic Caribbean and to focus on other areas of global confrontation, such as Central America and the Middle East. However, this shift has been characterized by policies that ignore socioeconomic factors—a potential cause of political outburst—and by an emphasis on predominantly military solutions that may be effective only in the short term. The economic vulnerability of microstates casts doubts on solutions dictated by strategic interests and implemented by mechanisms that require greater involvement by military and intelligence agencies. Though such measures may have the effect of deflecting global rivalries, they may also cause a delay in confronting the social problems affecting the Caribbean. In practice, this solution only succeeds in deferring the neccessity to address these focal points of internal political and social tensions—tensions that may eventually re-emerge in the context of new international conditions or the accumulation of internal factors.

From this perspective, the microstates in the region continue to be vulnerable, despite recent attempts at stabilization promoted by extraregional agents.

Notes

1. Alma Young and Dion Phillips (eds.): *Militarization in the Non-Hispanic Caribbean,* Boulder, Colo.: Lynne Rienner, 1986, p. 3.
2. Idem.
3. See David Simmons: "Militarization in the Caribbean: Concerns for National and Regional Security," in *International Journal,* 40 (1985).
4. See Tony Thorndike: "The Militarization of the Commonwealth Caribbean," paper presented at the Annual Convention of the British International Studies Association, Aberystwyth, December 1987.
5. Maingot: "Cuba and the Commonwealth Caribbean," p. 25.
6. Andres Serbin: "Crisis política e intervenciôn militar en Grenada," in *El Nacional,* Caracas, 31 October 1983, p. 7.
7. Simmons: "Militarization," p. 366.
8. Thorndike: "Militarization," p. 12.
9. International Institute for Strategic Studies: *The Military Balance,* pp. 192 and 197.
10. Ibid.
11. Thorndike: "Militarization," p. 11.
12. International Institute for Strategic Studies: *The Military Balance,* p. 198.
13. See Andres Serbin: *Nacionalismo, etnicidad y política en Guyana,* Caracas: Bruguera, 1981.
14. See Simmons: "Militarization;" and Maingot: "Cuba and the Commonwealth Caribbean."
15. See Andres Serbin: "Guyana: Socialismo, etnicidad e ideología nacional," *Politeia,* 8 (1979).
16. Danns: "The Role of the Military in Guyana," pp. 113–114.
17. Ibid., pp. 115–120.
18. International Institute for Strategic Studies: *The Military Balance,* p. 199.
19. Idem.
20. Danns: "The Role of the Military in Guyana," p. 116.
21. Alma Young: "The Central American Crisis and its Impact on Belize," in *Militarization in the Non-Hispanic Caribbean,* edited by Alma Young and Dion Phillips, Boulder, Colo.: Lynne Rienner, 1986, pp. 96–97.
22. Ibid.
23. Ibid.
24. Betty Sedoc-Dahlberg: "Interest Groups and the Military Regime in Suriname," in *Militarization in the Non-Hispanic Caribbean,* edited by Alma Young and Dion Phillips, Boulder, Colo.: Lynne Rienner, 1986, pp. 96–97.
25. Ibid.

26. International Institute for Strategic Studies: *The Military Balance,* p. 197.
27. Idem.
28. Sedoc-Dahlberg: "Interest Groups," pp. 96–97.
29. Payne et al.: *Grenada,* p. 84.
30. Ibid.
31. Ken Boodhoo: "Violence and Militarization in the Eastern Caribbean: The Case of Grenada," in *Militarization in the Non-Hispanic,* p. 81; Thorndike (1987) estimates 2,000 troops.
32. See Thorndike: "Militarization."
33. Payne et al.: *Grenada,* p. 84.
34. See Tony Thorndike: *Grenada: Politics, Economics and Safety,* London: Frances Pinter, 1985.
35. Payne et al.: *Grenada,* p. 86.
36. Bernard Diederich: "The End of West Indian Innocence," in *Caribbean Review,* 13, 2 (1984), p. 10.
37. Thorndike: "Militarization," p. 9.
38. See Diederich: "The End of West Indian Innocence," Thorndike and Lewis, "Prospect for a Regional Security System."
39. See Harden: *Small Is Dangerous.*
40. Lewis: "Prospect for a Regional Security System," p. 13.
41. Ibid.
42. Dion Phillips: "The Increasing Emphasis on Security and Defense in the Eastern Caribbean," in *Militarization in the Non-Hispanic,* p. 45.
43. See Harden: *Small Is Dangerous;* and Thorndike: "The Militarization."
44. *The Guardian,* 22 July 1986.
45. *Latin American Regional Report-Caribbean,* February 1987.
46. Ibidem.
47. *Latin American Regional Report-Caribbean,* March, 1987.
48. Young: "The Central American Crisis," p. 151.
49. *Newsweek,* 23 March 1988.
50. See Serbin: *Etnicidad.*
51. *Latin American Regional Report-Caribbean,* March 1987.
52. See Anthony Maingot: "Problems of a Transition to Democracy in Haiti," paper presented to the Royal Institute of International Affairs, London, January 1988.
53. Simmons: "Militarization," p. 357.
54. Maingot: "Problems of a Transition to Democracy," p. 18.
55. Thorndike: *Grenada,* p. 16.
56. Ibid.
57. Phillips: "The Increasing Emphasis on Security," p. 49.
58. See Harden: *Small Is Dangerous.*
59. See Robert Pastor: "The Impact of Grenada on the Caribbean: Ripples from a Revolution?" in *Latin America and Caribbean Record, 1983–1984,* edited by Jack W. Hopkins, New York: Holmes and Meier, 1985.
60. See Table 3.2.
61. See Harden: *Small Is Dangerous.*
62. See Maingot: "Problems of a Transition to Democracy;" and Thorndike: *Grenada.*
63. See Thorndike: *Grenada.*
64. Child: "Issues for U.S. Policy," pp. 145–153; and Ronfeldt, "Rethinking the Monroe Doctrine," p. 687.
65. Ibid.
66. See Jaramillo: "Problemas de seguridad."

67. See Maingot: "Problems of a Transition to Democracy."
68. See Phillips: "The Increasing Emphasis on Security."
69. Rodríguez Beruff: "Puerto Rico," pp. 76–77; and Child: "Issues for U.S. Policy," p. 152.
70. Barry et al.: *The Other Side of Paradise,* p. 201.
71. See Table 3.2.
70. Barry et al.: *The Other Side of Paradise,* p. 200.
73. Cintrón Tyriakian: "The Military and Security," pp. 56–59.
74. J. Ciricione: "The United States Navy in the Caribbean," in *Naval Forces,* 7, 3 (1986), p. 86.
75. See Greene and Scowcroft: *Western Interests.*
76. González: "The Cuban and Soviet Challenge," p. 90.
77. Pastor: "Cuba and the Soviet Union," p. 200.
78. Rebour and Trehard: "Signification strategique," p. 26.
79. González: "The Cuban and Soviet Challenge," p. 90; and International Institute for Strategic Studies: *The Military Balance,* p. 187.
80. Child: "Issues for U.S. Policy," p. 157.
81. González: "The Cuban and Soviet Challenge," p. 99; and International Institute for Strategic Studies: *The Military Balance,* p. 187.
82. Ciricione: "The United States Navy."
83. Ibid., pp. 84–92.
84. Quoted in Harden: *Small Is Dangerous.*
85. Martinez Sotomayor: *El Nuevo Caribe,* p. 273.
86. Ibid., p. 255.
87. Harden: *Small Is Dangerous,* p. 19.
88. Ibid.
89. See Commonwealth Secretariat: *Vulnerability.*
90. Ibid.
91. Ibid.
92. Quoted in Emmanuel: "Independence and Viability"
93. See Colin Clarke and Tony Payne (eds.): *Politics, Security and Development in Small States,* London: Allen and Unwin, 1987.
94. See Harden: *Small Is Dangerous.*
95. See Sutton: "Political Aspects."
96. Ibid.
97. See Espíndola: "Security Dilemmas."
98. See Commonwealth Secretariat: *Vulnerability.*

4
In Search of Peace

The debate that has surfaced once more in regard to establishing a peace zone in the Caribbean requires consideration of several factors. First and foremost, possibilities for denuclearization of the region must be evaluated. In addition, numerous precedents should be noted that indicate the willingness of some regional and extraregional actors to promote the establishment of a peace zone. A preliminary assessment of the possibilities here necessarily implies as well an adequate definition of the factors at work and an examination of the impact of Latin America on this initiative. Our assessment will also be based on the analysis presented in preceding chapters on regional and extraregional actors participating in the militarization and arms buildup in the region.

Denuclearization of the Caribbean

When studying the possibility of turning the Caribbean into a peace zone, it is important to consider the existing agreements relating to denuclearization of the region. A first step in this direction should be to study the effects of the Tlatelolco Treaty in the area.

The Treaty for the Prohibition of Nuclear Weapons in Latin America was signed in Mexico City on 14 February 1967. It is the first and only treaty establishing a nuclear weapons–free zone in a densely populated region. Most Latin American and Caribbean states have subscribed to it, and it was ratified by the world powers in Protocols I and II.

This process was not achieved without difficulties, some of which are of strictly regional scope. In 1965, the United States declared that neither the Virgin Islands nor Puerto Rico could be included in a treaty of this type, because the Virgin Islands are part of U.S. territory and because of Puerto Rico's special relationship with it.[1] France also delayed its decision to ratify Additional Protocol I until such time as the treaty itself was ratified.[2] To these delays and reluctance must be added the hesitations of those states in the region that felt the treaty could infringe upon their own expectations in regard to nuclear development or security. This was the case in Argentina and Cuba. The latter has yet to join the treaty, despite the fact that its nuclear activities are covered by IAEA safeguards.[3] The Treaty of Tlatelolco is applicable to thirty-three independent states in Latin America and the Caribbean and to the territories of France, the Netherlands, Great Britain, and the United States in the region. By 1 May 1985, it had been ratified by twenty-three states in the region. In the Caribbean these included Antigua and Barbuda, Bahamas, Barbados, Dominican Republic, Grenada, Haiti, Jamaica, Suriname, and Trinidad and Tobago. Guyana and Belize have not been invited to sign the treaty, owing to their border disputes with other Latin American countries. Cuba, Dominica, St. Lucia, St. Kitts-Nevis, and St. Vincent and the Grenadines have not signed the treaty, the latter four because of their recent independence. The French DOMS are also excluded from the treaty.[4]

Agreements signed by the United States and the Soviet Union have frozen, for the time being, the possibility of establishing nuclear bases in Cuba. After the Cuban missile crisis in 1962, the USSR agreed to withdraw its strategic arms from the island in exchange for assurances by the United States that it would not intervene militarily in Cuba.[5] Nevertheless, as described in Chapter 3, both superpowers maintain installations in the region with the capability for strategic nuclear development; in the Soviet case, in Cuba, and in the case of the United States, primarily in Puerto Rico.[6] Some analysts believe that there is no possibility of nuclear confrontation in the area; however, superpower capabilities for reinforcing their strategic nuclear offensive are still in place.[7]

Background to Peace Zone Efforts

One of the first leaders to promote conversion of the region into a peace zone was Eric Williams, who stated, in an address to the Trinidad and Tobago House of Representatives in December 1963, "If there is any justice in heaven, the area which has the just claim to being declared a zone of peace is the Caribbean area, which has for so long been afflicted by the machinations and maneuvers, the hot wars and the cold wars, of the great powers and superpowers."[8] This proposal was furthered by a number of scholars who developed a concept of *pacem in maribus* applicable to the region.[9]

Another leader of Eric Williams' own generation, Cheddi Jagan, expressed an aspiration prevalent among the left-wing sectors of the Caribbean political elite. He stressed, "Peace is necessary to halt the arms race, to divert funds for development, to save detente and to ensure peaceful cooperation on a global scale."[10]

Supporting the establishment of peace zones in general, the action program contained in the Final Document of the UN Special Session on

Disarmament includes the following statement:

> 64. The establishment of zones of peace in various regions of the world under appropriate conditions to be clearly defined and determined freely by the States concerned in the zone, taking into account the characteristics of the zone and the principles of the Charter of the United Nations, and in conformity with international law, can contribute to strengthening the security of states within such zones and to international peace and security as a whole.[11]

Establishment of a peace zone in the Caribbean was formally proposed by Grenada in October 1979 during the Twelfth Plenary Session of the General Assembly of the Organization of American States, held in La Paz. A resolution was approved on that occasion vis-à-vis the security situation in the Caribbean, characterized at that time by superpower military and political activities and the hiring of mercenaries to destabilize or overthrow constitutional governments. The resolution was aimed at repudiating a perception of the region as a sphere of influence of any power, stressing support for ideological pluralism and peaceful coexistence and appealing to all states to recognize the region as a peace zone.[12]

The English-speaking Caribbean states fully supported the resolution, particularly Grenada, which was then subject to increasing destabilizing pressure from the United States, and Guyana, which was concerned that Venezuela might carry out a military offensive to take over the Esequibo territory. Grenada and Dominica were particularly concerned about several coup attempts that had been carried out by mercenaries.[13] The United States, however, ignored the resolution and it was therefore never implemented, despite the fact that it had been approved by the OAS General Assembly.

The original idea was nevertheless taken up again by the foreign affairs ministers of the CARICOM member states during their Sixth Meeting, held in Grenada from 30 June to 1 July 1981. A working group was subsequently formed, which met in Belize in March 1982.[14] The organization's summit conference in Ocho Ríos, Jamaica, also promoted the work of this group and analyzed the possible options for a regional security treaty, linked to the establishment of a peace zone. Nevertheless, despite such backing, no further action has been taken.[15] The initiative falls within the framework of the principles of nonintervention and ideological pluralism promoted by CARICOM and later reaffirmed by other countries in the region; these principles, however, were challenged by the Grenada invasion.

The initial proposals that were put forward by Grenada during the Belize meeting merit consideration:

1. Adherence to the principle of: a) non-interference; and b) the peaceful solution of disputes;

2. Strengthening of ties of good neighbourliness and cooperation within the region;
3. The right of all peoples to choose their own political, economic and social system free from all forms of outside dictation and pressure;
4. The right to develop relations with Governments of different political orientation based on ideological pluralism and peaceful coexistence;
5. The need to strengthen and deepen existing economic, technical, scientific and cultural ties among states in the region;
6. The right of states of the region to develop and utilise their natural and national resources and wealth for the benefit and in the interest of the peoples of the region;
7. The need to secure better terms of trade for the countries of the region;
8. Termination of colonial status and foreign domination of all territories in the region;
9. Prohibition of establishment of new foreign military or naval bases in the region and dismantling of such bases where they exist against the wishes of the countries of the region;
10. Prohibition of the use of international and regional financial institutions and bilateral and multilateral financial and economic assistance programmes as a means of exerting pressure or coercion on countries of the region;
11. Prohibition of propaganda or diplomatic intervention as a means of intervening in the internal affairs of countries of the region;
12. Prohibition of financing, recruitment and training and the use of mercenaries as well as any facility, support or assistance given to them for the purpose of intervening in the internal affairs of Governments in the region;
13. Prohibition of all military and naval maneuvers and exercises of an aggressive or provocative nature;
14. Acknowledgment of the validity and right of peaceful and unobstructed freedom of navigation and flight over waters of the region in accordance with the rules and principles of international law and custom; and
15. Prohibition of the installation or continual maintenance of nuclear weapons in territories in the region under the control or administration of nuclear powers.[16]

This document has been quoted extensively herein to reflect the concern of a Caribbean microstate in the face of various threats to its security from outside the region.

In addition to the position of some governments and political leaders favoring the establishment of a peace zone in the Caribbean, other sectors have expressed their support of the initiative. In April 1982, the Caribbean Conference of Churches (CCC), which groups the various religious denominations in the region and publishes the influential monthly *Caribbean Contact*, adopted a resolution appealing to CARICOM to consider the establishment of a peace zone in the Caribbean and the ratification of whatever treaty might be necessary to achieve this goal.[17] A CCC assembly has reiterated this position, in response to militarization in the region resulting from the presence of the superpowers and the impact of the Central American crisis on Caribbean societies. The position taken by the CCC meeting, held in Barbados in 1986, was supported by Prime Minister Errol Barrow, who criticized the United States for attempting to turn the Caribbean states into client-states with some access to U.S. goods and markets, and the USSR as well for attempting to Afghanize the region and to use the Caribbean as a missile base in the event of superpower confrontation.[18]

Barrow's position reflected the fact that he and other Caribbean leaders, among them James "Sonny" Mitchell in St. Vincent, questioned the attempt to establish a security force in the area. Their position marks a true return, in the wake of events in Grenada, to the principles of nonalignment, ideological pluralism, and nonintervention traditionally advocated by CARICOM.

The proposal for a peace zone in the Caribbean was also recommended by the UK Foreign Affairs Committee in a report on Central America and the Caribbean prepared for the House of Commons in 1982. It appears from this report that during its preparation the committee made efforts to ascertain the degree of receptivity in certain sectors of the Jamaican and Trinidad and Tobago governments to the idea of a peace zone. In Trinidad and Tobago, both the ruling PNM, adhering to the traditionally favorable attitude of its mentor Eric Williams, and the opposition parties expressed their willingness to take a more active role in promoting a peace zone in the Caribbean. Thus, among its recommendations, the report proposes that the United Kingdom foster greater awareness of the concept of a peace zone in the Caribbean.[19]

The Venezuelan government has also reiterated the need to declare the Caribbean a peace zone. This is a position that has been assumed by both major political parties.[20]

Establishment of a Peace Zone in the Caribbean: A Preliminary Assessment

It can be concluded that the arms race and militarization processes in the region have had two main causes. First and foremost, they reflect the impact of global conflict in the area. Second, and to a much lesser extent, they can also be traced to the effects of as yet unresolved border conflicts, which are often a factor in justifying the development of armed forces.

The impact of the East-West confrontation—the principle reason for increased militarization by countries in the region as well as for the increasing military presence of extraregional actors—predominantly reflects the geopolitical needs of the United States to ensure its "sphere of influence" in the region, to the exclusion of all potentially hostile extrahemispheric actors. This sphere of influence had begun to take shape historically before the emergence of the current superpower conflict and it has been particularly intensified since the progressive withdrawal of the United Kingdom from the region. The geostrategic need of the United States to strengthen its southern flank surpasses its strictly economic and political interests in the Caribbean. It is true that confrontation with the USSR could threaten U.S. access to the region's mineral resources, particularly petroleum and bauxite, and to its sealanes, including the Panama Canal. A primary motivation for the "sphere of influence" policy, however, lies in the desire of the United States to uphold its political influence in the Caribbean and to preserve the area as a symbol of its capacity to expand hegemonically to other regions in the defense of its national interests.[21]

Within this framework, events in Grenada constituted a crisis for the Reagan administration, in view of the political situation in Central America and the administration's adherence to the ideological and political principles inherent in the objective of containing "Soviet expansionism."

From this perspective, Grenada posed a threat to U.S. interests in the region both strategically, because it increased the range of Cuban-Soviet influence, already based in Nicaragua and growing in El Salvador and Suriname as well, and because it represented a model of political and social organization associated with a development strategy that questioned U.S. hegemony in the Caribbean. Over time, expansion of this model implied the emergence of social alternatives that could become expressions of antagonism toward the U.S. "sphere of influence" in the region.

It should be noted that USSR participation in this process was not effective; its objective vis-à-vis Grenada was to generate a focal point for deflection of U.S. strategic resources, rather than to assure its own sphere of influence in the region. The absence of a Soviet policy—in either political or military terms—to reinforce the Grenadan process fully illustrates the situation.[22]

As already mentioned, these objectives did not coincide with those of Cuba, which hoped to break its regional isolation and establish alliances in the non-Hispanic Caribbean. However, as a function of the "surrogate thesis," to the extent that Cuba was perceived as an actor adhering to Soviet interests in the region, it was identified with these interests. Ultimately, the Grenadan crisis was fundamentally another chapter in the U.S. confrontation with Cuba begun in the 1960s.

It should also be noted that the detonating factor for increased U.S. military presence in the island Caribbean and for its final intervention in Grenada was this confrontation, compounded with Central American events, rather than other destabilization phenomena, such as operations by organized crime or drug trafficking, which had not as yet provoked actions of this magnitude.

In this context, the United States stimulated the hopes of the conservative governments, which had come to power in the region at the time, for eliminating the potential threat to their interests and objectives in the Caribbean. However, shortly after the Grenada intervention, the area once again ceased to be a priority for U.S. strategic objectives.[23] Some analysts have accurately pointed out that this policy repeated a traditional U.S. pattern—focal intervention in reaction to a crisis, followed by policies that are guided in another direction once the crisis has subsided.[24]

Once "stabilization" was achieved in the region after the Grenada invasion, the establishment of a regional security force, such as Tom Adams and other conservative leaders had advocated, was no longer justified. Additionally, economic assistance channeled through the CBI was redefined. The arms race and growth of the armed forces in certain non-Hispanic Caribbean states declined as in the cases of Jamaica and Trinidad. Within this framework, the CARICOM governments tended once again, as they had in the past, to take up moderate positions and aspire to a nonaligned foreign policy. The regional approach was again emphasized for solving chronic socioeconomic Caribbean problems. In general, a more pronounced unwillingness to participate in the East-West confrontation emerged, evidenced by attempts to reinforce regional initiatives through CARICOM and to strengthen cooperation and technical assistance ties with Canada, Latin America, and their former colonial metropolitan centers. Furthermore, as the effective military influence of Cuba waned, pragmatic positions were assumed vis-à-vis the United States as a decisive regional geopolitical factor. This attitude is characteristic not only of certain sectors among the Caribbean political elites, but among some left-wing groupings in the region as well.[25]

After the Grenadan crisis, the need arose for a new approach to deal with regional security, which would prevent excessive dependence on U.S. military assistance while also ensuring that events such as those that had led to the crisis would never again occur. This approach renewed the traditional stress placed by the political elites in the English-speaking Caribbean on coordinating a regional security policy with promotion of economic development and consolidation of democratic systems. The concern for implementing economic development strategies appropriate to the characteristics of the Caribbean states is not an approach exclusive to CARICOM; it is particularly to be found among the political elites in the more developed English-speaking Caribbean countries.

At the political level, in the context of the English-speaking Caribbean, this perspective is related to the conviction that the political system inspired by the Whitehall and Westminster model continues to be the most appropriate for stabilizing and consolidating democracy in the region. However, adherence to this point of view makes it difficult for countries not originating in the British colonial sphere to join CARICOM. Moreover, the desire to return to a basically nonaligned foreign policy, preserving the greatest possible distance from the effects of global confrontation, again became evident in the English-speaking Caribbean states and was reactivated after the "conservative tide" of the early 1980s. Autonomy and regional cooperation, traditionally advocated by the political elites that led the gradual decolonization process in the Commonwealth Caribbean,[26] were again urged. Significantly, this return to the ideas of Eric Williams, Errol Barrow, and Michael Manley, among others, also produced a shift in attitude toward the Latin American countries, which are gradually assuming a more important role in the Caribbean.

Promotion of a peace zone in the Caribbean seeks not only to prevent situations such as the Grenada invasion, with its attendant consequences for the region, but also to eliminate the possibility of other conflicts, particularly with those Latin American countries that have border disputes with some non-Hispanic Caribbean states.

The European countries perceive the idea of a peace zone as a viable direction for ensuring stabilization of the Caribbean, eliminating existing security problems, facilitating the flow of regional resources, and strengthening efforts toward solving the problems generated by socioeconomic development—which is considered to be the principal Caribbean problem. This is the position of some sectors, at any rate, in Great Britain, France, and the Netherlands; in the wake of democratization processes experienced by some countries in the region, it is shared as well by the Socialist International (SI) and the American Christian Democrat Organization (ODCA).

The Latin American countries, in turn, view the possibility of establishing a peace zone in the area as a significant response to their regional situation within the framework of North-South relations, offering one possibility for guaranteeing stability and leading to the defense of their vital interests in the region. The improvement in relations between Venezuela and Guyana and the decision to solve the border conflict via UN mechanisms, as well as the agreement by Guatemala and Belize to form a commission to end their territorial dispute, are conducive to the eventual willingness of all parties to assure peace in the region.[27]

Latin American support of the peace initiative may be hindered by a perception of the Cuban presence as a threat to national interests, particularly in the cases of Venezuela, Colombia, and Brazil. The evolution of the Cuban situation in the Latin American environment, however—for example, with the willingness expressed by the Group of Eight to seek Cuba's renewed participation in the Latin American community—may indicate that this obstacle may be overcome in the short term.

It is also possible to achieve denuclearization of the area if, on one hand, Cuba joins the Tlatelolco Treaty, and, on the other, the United States accepts the political stabilization of the region, recognizing the significant changes brought about by the increasing autonomy of the regional actors and the Latin American states.

The process of partial militarization of the region as a result of U.S. policy vis-à-vis Cuba and Grenada, which may have at first seemed irreversible, now appears to be controllable if adequate mechanisms are put in place, providing that at the regional level critical situations such as arose in Grenada are not repeated. Nevertheless, severe socioeconomic problems persist in the region, including rising unemployment rates combined with an explosive population increase in the younger sectors most affected by unemployment, and increasing external indebtedness coupled with a decrease in resources. The lack of specific strategies for solving these problems may give rise to new radicalization processes, including those identified with previous unsuccessful experiences in the region.

The recommendations proposed by Grenada at the Belize meeting, quoted extensively earlier in this chapter, may serve as a guide to the establishment of a peace zone in the region, assuming the effective support of the Latin American states, and their adherence to the fundamental principles, traditionally promoted by the Latin American community, of nonintervention and peaceful settlement of conflicts. However, the Grenadan document also mentions obstacles deriving from the presence of extraregional actors in the region, which are extremely difficult to overcome in the short term. The presence of these actors hinders the achievement of such goals as the elimination of colonial status, of foreign domination in all Caribbean territories, and of economic pressures as destabilization mechanisms. To these difficulties should be added the inability of the Caribbean states thus far to effectively implement their basic aspiration of greater regional cooperation, either within CARICOM or in relationship to the Latin American countries.

Echoing the basic points of the Grenadan document, Carlos Portales has pointed out that the process of establishing a peace zone in the Caribbean essentially requires four fundamental measures: (1) the withdrawal of all military forces and bases of extraregional actors; (2) implementation of a denuclearization process; (3) implementation of a regional policy for arms control and disarmament; and (4) acceptance of a peace zone status for the region by the world powers.[28]

The principal obstacles to implementation of these four measures lie in the reluctance of the United States to reduce its influence and control over regional security, in the reluctance of the Latin American countries engaged in border disputes with Caribbean states to weaken their military positions and—even if these obstacles were to be overcome in the long run—in the difficulties for implementation of adequate mechanisms for turning the Caribbean into a peace zone.

It can therefore be concluded that, in light of the Central American crisis and its interpretation in terms of global confrontation with the USSR, the United States will be very unlikely—at least in the short term and until it has completely asserted its regional hegemony—to accept a peace zone in an area whose influence it considers vital for strategic reasons as well as prestige. Intense disarmament negotiations and stabilization of influence by both superpowers in the Third World, coupled with the formulation of a new policy toward the region as a result of the crisis of consensus prevailing in the United States, could alter this situation, if only partially. Pressure would most likely be required from other countries, particularly extraregional actors. Relevant factors here involve the willingness of the USSR to abandon its installations and troops in Cuba, and Cuba's willingness to accept a disarmament process that could in the long run leave it defenseless before a U.S. threat. The shift in Soviet policy toward the region and the Third World in general, in the context of the withdrawal from Afghanistan and the U.S. proposal that both parties suspend arms shipments to Central America,[29] allows for optimism in regard to a favorable Soviet attitude toward declaring a peace zone in the Caribbean.[30] The Cuban attitude may be conditioned by various factors related to its internal political processes. However, the possibility of demilitarization in Cuban society and reallocation of resources to meet other pressing needs, together with a guarantee that all military activity would cease, could stimulate a positive attitude toward the peace zone initiative, particularly in view of the new regional willingness to renew Cuba's participation in the Latin American community. In any case, the Cuban position should be assessed in relation to increasing differences with the internal process of the Soviet Union and its foreign policy toward the Third World, as well as recent internal developments.

Relative to the obstacles posed by the impact of global conflict in the region, the second obstacle to the establishment of a peace zone—unresolved border conflicts in the area—may be more easily surmounted. Though they have not advanced in any significant way, Venezuelan efforts to solve the Esequibo dispute have nevertheless led to improved relations with Guyana. A similar situation can be observed in regard to improved relations between Guatemala and Belize.[31] Despite the encouraging signs, however, neither conflict seems likely to be solved in the short or medium term. Border conflicts also persist between Venezuela and Trinidad, Venezuela and Colombia, and Guyana and Suriname, to name the most salient, which could dash any hopes of a disarmament process; the same can be said for relations between Haiti and the Dominican Republic.

Moreover, despite the consequences of the Grenada crisis, Cuba continues to be a source of concern not only to the United States but also to Latin American states, such as Colombia and Venezuela. These concerns are rooted both in internal political processes and in a preoccupation with ensuring political stability in the region as a whole. Nonetheless, implementation of a peace zone in South America could be a positive factor for setting into motion a similar process in the Caribbean. Likewise, in the long run, a resolution of the Central American crisis may create adequate conditions for nearby extraregional actors, such as the United States and the Latin American countries, to accept establishment of a peace zone in the region.

Reciprocally, establishment of a peace zone in the Caribbean would facilitate implementation of a similar initiative in South America, where the principal obstacles lie in the persistence of intraregional conflicts. A peace zone in the Caribbean, furthermore, would contribute to strengthening relations between the region and the Latin American states, not only at the level of economic cooperation, but also in relation to modalities for political coordination that would lead to greater bargaining power for both regions at the international level.

Although of lesser importance than the two obstacles mentioned above, consideration must also be given to the possible attitude of the former colonial metropolitan centers. In this regard, Great Britain, the Netherlands, and France should be studied as separate problems, despite the fact that they ratified the Tlatelolco Treaty. While the Netherlands is looking forward to withdrawing from the region, Great Britain continues to be present in its associated dependencies. The persistence of the Malvinas (Falklands) conflict requires a hardly negotiable British strategic presence in the Caribbean. For the duration of the Guatemala and Belize conflict, Great Britain will also maintain a military, albeit limited and partial, contingent in Belize or, at most, would accept that it be substituted by some form of U.S. presence. The maintenance of French bases and troops, in turn, is closely related to France's strategic interests in French Guiana (which also implies an interest on the part of European states linked to the Arianne aerospace project) and to the fact that it does not belong to NATO's Strategic Command; these circumstances are unlikely to change and are basically dependent upon France's participation in the global system.

Finally, in addition to the degree of support forthcoming from these extraregional actors, a major problem in regard to the establishment of a peace zone in the Caribbean lies in the question of its design and implementation by a regional or international organization that can guarantee and control its operation. We will outline briefly some existing alternatives.

In view of previous efforts of the United Nations to address issues in other regions of the world, it does not seem likely that this issue could be framed in that context independently of the political weight exercised by each of the superpowers within the organization. Implementation of this initiative should necessarily be considered an aspiration within the framework of North-South relations rather than East-West confrontation.[32]

Despite its willingness to take on the role of a guarantor body, expressed in a 1979 resolution, the OAS can hardly be called upon to do so, given its recent crisis and persisting U.S. influence within it.

The most appropriate organization to oversee implementation of the initiative would be CARICOM, particularly if we bear in mind its previous experience in coordinating the foreign policies of Caribbean Community states. However, non-English-speaking Caribbean countries are accepted only as observers in this organization, and the requests by Haiti, Suriname, and the Dominican Republic for accession remain unanswered. The lack of effective participation by non-English-speaking states would make problematic CARICOM's role as an executing agency and, moreover, would even create difficulties in defining clearly the area to be covered by the peace zone.

The mechanisms to be implemented in order effectively to convert the Caribbean into a peace zone must be considered carefully if the problems experienced in creating a similar zone in the Indian Ocean are to be avoided.[33] Moreover, from a geopolitical viewpoint, it must be taken into account that the region is often perceived in the light of contradictory national, regional, and hemispheric interests.

In this context, existing obstacles can only be overcome, both at the regional and international levels, by the political will and coordinated action of the principal actors involved in the initiative, the Caribbean states themselves. However, achievement of such coordination demands a shared awareness that resolution of regional security issues first requires solutions to basic socioeconomic problems, which are the main cause of the political instability and vulnerability of Caribbean societies. By the same token, appropriate strategies for overcoming these problems will have to be developed both independently and through regional coordination.

Notes

1. Miguel Marín Bosch: "The Treaty of Tlatelolco and the NPY," in *Nuclear Non-Proliferation and Global Security,* edited by David B. Dewitt, London: Croom Helm, 1987, p. 176.
2. Ibid.
3. Josef Goldblat: *Nuclear Non-Proliferation: A Guide to the Debate,* London: Taylor and Francis, 1985, p. 36.
4. Bosch: "The Treaty of Tlatelolco," pp. 177–178.
5. Greene and Scowcroft: *Western Interests,* p. 11.
6. See Proyecto Caribeño de Justicia y Paz: *Puerto Rico ante la Guerra Nuclear,* Dossier No. 5, January–February 1985.
7. See Sutton: "Political Aspects."
8. Eric Williams: "The Foreign Relations of Trinidad and Tobago," address by the Honorable Dr. Eric Williams on 6 December 1963.
9. See Rubin: "La Cuenca del Caribe."
10. Cheddi Jagan: *The Caribbean: Whose Backyard?* n.p., n.d., p. 132.
11. Quoted in Ibid.
12. Simmons: "Militarization," p. 372.
13. Ibid.
14. Jagan: *The Caribbean,* p. 313.
15. Harden: *Small Is Dangerous,* p. 167.
16. Jagan: *The Caribbean,* pp. 313–314.
17. Ibid.
18. *Latin American Regional Report-Caribbean,* October 1986, p. 5.
19. See Foreign Affairs Committee: *Caribbean and Central America: Report to the House of Commons,* United Kingdom Parliament, 1983.

20. See José Rodríguez Iturbe: "El área vital para la seguridad y defensa y la política exterior venezolana," in *La Agenda de la Política Exterior de Venezuela,* Caracas: UCV, 1983, and *El Caribe: Elementos para una reflexión política a fines de los 80,* Caracas: Centauro, 1987. Also, statements by Venezuelan Foreign Minister Dr. Simón Alberto Consoalvi in a communiqué issued after the visit to the Dominican Republic, in October 1985, in which he expresses the Venezuelan aspiration that the Caribbean be converted into a peace zone. More recently, during a visit to Trinidad in August 1989, President Carlos Andrés Pérez stressed the need to declare the Caribbean a peace zone (*El Nacional,* 4 October 1989, front page).

21. See Sutton: "Political Aspects."

22. See Jiri and Virginia Valenta: "Leninism in Grenada," in *Problems of Communism,* 33 (July–August 1984).

23. See Heine: "Status aparte."

24. See Jack Child: "Variables para la política de Estados Unidos en la Cuenca del Caribe en la década de 1980: Seguridad," in *Intereses occidentales y política de Estados Unidos en el Caribe,* edited by James Greene and Brent Scowcroft, Buenos Aires: Grupo Editor Latinoamericano, 1985.

25. See Serbin: *Etnicidad.*

26. See Carlos Portales: "Zona de Paz: una alternativa a los desafíos estratégicos de América Latina," *Cuadernos Semestrales,* FLACSO, 15 (1984).

27. See Andres Serbin and Jacinto Castillo: *Conflictos limítrofes y proceso democrático en Venezuela,* Santiago: ILET, 1985.

28. See Portales: "Zona de paz."

29. *Caribbean Insight,* April 1988.

30. *The Economist,* 9–15 April 1988, and *Newsweek,* 18 April 1988.

31. See A. Glinkin, N. Isakova, and P. Yakovlev: *América Latina contra el peligro de guerra,* Moscow: Novosti, 1987.

32. See John Barton: *The Politics of Peace,* Stanford: Stanford University Press, 1981.

33. Ibid.

5
Caribbean Geopolitics and Global Change

When the Spanish version of this book was published in 1988, events worldwide were reshaping the international system as we had known it in the 1980s. Now, two years later, these changes are having a direct bearing on the insertion of the Caribbean in this system and will have a decisive influence on the possibilities for peace in the region. For this reason, a postscript to update the book seems justified, even if only to outline the region's general characteristics as a new decade begins.

Transformation in the International System

World trade and production underwent rapid restructuring in the 1980s, as increasing globalization of the world economy led to the elimination of national boundaries in the process of capitalist accumulation at the world level. Global restructuring has been associated with a technological revolution that has paved the way for the growing influence of biotechnology, robotics, and computers. The relative value of agricultural products and raw materials has, however, declined and been affected by the increasingly protectionist practices of a set of economic blocs around which the dynamics of the world economy is beginning to revolve.

While the European Economic Community advances toward integration in 1992, North America has tended to become a free trade zone, forming a bloc that is gradually integrating the U.S. economy with those of Canada and Mexico, and that anticipates the future incorporation of the Caribbean Basin. A new economic bloc, centered in Japan and its East Asian and Southeast Asian partners and competitors, is also emerging in the Pacific Basin. To some analysts, this process and its progressive economic association with the U.S. West Coast will cause a gradual shift in the world economic axis from the Atlantic to the Pacific.

The Soviet Union, together with Eastern Europe, has been joining the process of global economic restructuring and hopes to participate increasingly in the accompanying technological and industrial revolution.

However, within the framework of the global process, it is obvious that the boundaries between regions are unclear, porous, and sometimes overlapping,[1] as for example, in the case of the Pacific economies with the U.S. West Coast.

In the USSR, perestroika has brought with it significant political transformation in the sphere of international relations. In a world system that already had begun to assume a multipolar nature, political change in the Soviet Union and its effect on foreign policy has not only allowed for political changes in Eastern Europe that just a few years ago would have been unthinkable, but it has also resulted in an atmosphere of global détente and in a new Soviet policy toward the Third World in general and Latin America in particular.[2]

The gap between industrialized and Third World countries has, however, deepened, with the economic growth rate of the former continuing to increase while the external debt burden has plunged the latter into a profound economic crisis. Growth and development have come to a halt in much of the Third World, and in some countries substantially decreased. Latin America is one among the regions to have suffered the greatest impact on its economic position vis-à-vis developing countries and the developed world.[3] The social and political effects of the crisis are also cause for concern among the political elites, as evidenced by the UN General Assembly addresses of presidents Menem, Sarney, and Pérez.[4]

Within this general framework, the situation of the Caribbean Basin is also undergoing notable change, both because of its attempts to join the global process that is restructuring production—a process dominated by industrialized countries—and because of its strategic role in an international system gravitating toward détente and disarmament.

Global Change and the Caribbean

The new realities are leading the Caribbean Basin to form part of the North American economic conglomerate, with the Caribbean Basin Initiative as a key step in this direction. The raw materials traditionally produced by the region are becoming less important, as a result of changes in U.S. sugar policy and the surge in chemical substitutes for sugar, the drop in oil prices and world restructuring of the petrochemical industry, and the progressive replacement of the bauxite industry with plastic by-products.

The CBI focuses instead on promoting services such as tourism aimed at North American consumers and on creating free zones to stimulate exports of nontraditional products. The key role assigned to Puerto Rico, the "twin plant" projects through 936 funds, and other similar initiatives are contributing to the trend toward regional restructuring of production.[5]

This process should be seen in conjunction with consolidation of the

U.S. strategic and military presence in the subregion, through its military bases and through military assistance and cooperation agreements that were established with Caribbean countries after the Grenada invasion. Militarization of the region, which many analysts feared some years ago,[6] did not occur, but it is obvious that since the Grenada invasion—and more recently, the occupation of Panama—the Caribbean Basin clearly has been submerged into the sphere of U.S. influence.

Paradoxically, Soviet foreign policy has ascribed less and less importance to this sphere, both as a result of a shift in priorities in its Third World policy, where the stress currently lies in expanding Soviet economic relations, and because it has explicitly decided not to become involved in regional conflicts. Soviet support of the process of seeking a solution to the Central American conflict is ample illustration of this fact.[7]

The ever-increasing differences between Cuba and the Soviet Union in regard to this policy in no way affect global and regional détente. The Cuban influence in the Caribbean Basin, especially in the non-Hispanic Caribbean, has drastically diminished since the Grenadan crisis, while its hemispheric policy has been redirected toward the strengthening of ties with the Latin American community.

While the Cuban ideological influence has diminished at the regional level, the impact of U.S. economic initiatives and financial and political influence has been increasing in Puerto Rico, as has Puerto Rico's strategic and military importance. It is still not known, however, whether the 1991 referendum will in fact be held and what its consequences may be for the political future of the associated state.

Within this context, the "conservative pragmatism"[8] of the CARICOM governments fluctuates between adhering to the established regional scheme of things—a process of progressive assimilation into the North American economic conglomerate—and pressing on toward regional integration. The latter alternative, despite its limited economic scope, is perceived as a viable response to the consolidation of the increasingly centripetal world economic blocs. The CARICOM summit meeting held on 4 July 1989 issued the "Grand Anse Declaration," which urged member states to advance toward regional integration through a four-year program aimed at confronting "global economic changes."[9]

In March of the same year, at a Group of Eight meeting of foreign ministers, the representatives of Mexico, Venezuela, and Colombia expressed the willingness of their respective governments to study a regional integration scheme for the three countries, which would include assistance and cooperation programs with the Caribbean. This trilateral agreement would provide for exchange of information among the participating members in order to improve their cooperation with Central American and Caribbean countries. It also seeks to strengthen the Caribbean Development Bank and the Central

American Bank, and to establish various mechanisms for granting tariff preferences to the countries in the region.[10] The proposal continued to be on the agenda at meetings held by Mexico, Venezuela, and Colombia throughout the year. No specific initiative has as yet been launched, however, and current differences in the respective reaction of these countries to the U.S. invasion of Panama would first have to be overcome.

The true scope of such a proposal is difficult to envision. Priority objectives of both Mexico and Colombia in the Pacific Basin led in the 1970s and 1980s to significant shifts in their Caribbean policies and to a greater overlapping of the Mexican economy with that of the United States. The Venezuelan government, on the other hand, has been promoting its presence in the non-Hispanic Caribbean, with CARICOM relations as a priority item on its foreign policy agenda. Action by the Lusinchi administration has been followed up by the recent meeting of President Carlos Andrés Pérez with Prime Ministers Michael Manley, Erskine Sandford, A. N. R. Robinson, and James Mitchell, and with President Hoyte, in Tobago, on 5 August 1989. The Venezuelan initiative to join CARICOM as an observer nation is additional evidence of the country's intention to continue to promote cooperation between the non-Hispanic Caribbean and Latin America.[11]

This willingness, however, which CARICOM shares, is at odds with the region's general trend toward Caribbean integration with the North American economic conglomerate. The economic difficulties experienced by both the non-Hispanic Caribbean countries and the Latin American states also work against a renewal of the atmosphere of cooperation characterizing South-South relations in the 1970s, even though two of its principal sponsors, Michael Manley and Carlos Andrés Pérez, have reappeared on the scene.

Central America sheds no new and encouraging light on the situation. There, actors in the regional peace process, based on the Esquipulas and Tela accords, are grappling with the aftermath of the Panama invasion, intensification of the civil war in El Salvador, and the consequences of the Nicaraguan elections.

There is little doubt that the vital topic on the regional security agenda for the present decade will continue to be events in Central America. The East-West confrontation, however, will be replaced by the much more overwhelming issue of drug trafficking. The salience of this issue is evidenced by the fact that the U.S. government justified its invasion of Panama on drug trafficking allegations and that this issue is also at the root of its differences with Peru and Colombia; thus, this new priority of the Bush administration is the key security topic for the Latin American states as well.

Jamaican marijuana accounts for 15 percent of total marijuana consumption in the United States and is the third most important Jamaican export item and source of foreign currency;[12] similar figures are reported for Belize. The Bahamas and some British-associated territories are money-laundering havens. But the crux of the matter is that the area is a key link in drug routes from Latin America to the U.S. market. For example, the U.S. Drug Enforcement Agency estimates that between 60 and 80 percent of cocaine entering the United States crosses the Caribbean.[13]

Michael Manley's recent proposal to form a multinational force to control drug trafficking in the region should be seen in this light.[14] This proposal effectively supercedes the debate on formation of a regional security force that was initiated by some conservative governments in the early 1980s.

This general view of changes in the international system and their impact on the area points to new realities, leading to new scenarios for Caribbean evolution during the 1990s. The following outline of these scenarios will be limited, of course, by the usual uncertainties that accompany rapid change, and by any unforeseen reversals, deviations, or digressions that may occur in the global and regional system.

The 1990s: New Scenarios for Peace?

Given the tendency toward the development of economic blocs and the shifting priorities in U.S foreign policy that have led to consolidation of a geopolitical as well as economic U.S. "sphere of influence" in North America, the dominant trend is for the island Caribbean to gradually join the North American economic bloc. At the political and military levels, this process implies greater consolidation of the U.S. presence and increased U.S. influence and assistance in the non-Hispanic Caribbean; at the economic level, CBI I and II are instrumental, with Puerto Rico playing a key role in both. Moreover, upon implementation of EEC integration in 1992, any difficulties that may arise concerning exports, especially as regards rum and bananas, will tend to force the Caribbean to look to North America,[15] regardless of attempts to diversify its economic ties. At the same time, historical obstacles to cooperation as discussed in Chapters 1 and 4 and economic difficulties currently faced by Caribbean and Latin American states also stand in the way of their coming together in the short term.

Furthermore, the lack of infrastructures and capital, difficulties in exporting traditional products, and the obstacles to promoting industrial restructuring are causing the Caribbean economies to lean toward the production of services and the manufacture of nontraditional products in the free zones. These developments, occurring within the framework of CBI options, also assimilate the Caribbean into the North American economic conglomerate.

Consequently, although efforts to further CARICOM economic cooperation and integration and OECS political integration may be stepped up as a means for creating a united front vis-à-vis the major economic blocs, they are highly unlikely to succeed in halting the trend toward North American assimilation.

The bargaining power of the Caribbean states could improve, but this too would be a relative achievement, since CARICOM foreign policy coordination, though noteworthy, has probably reached a ceiling, particularly in view of recent setbacks experienced by Caribbean diplomacy in international organizations.[16]

In light of the resolution of the Grenadan episode and Cuba's weakening regional influence, the East-West confrontation is no longer the most appropriate framework for approaching the non-Hispanic Caribbean geopolitical situation. Though the East-West conflict may occasionally be relevant, it is of decreasing importance in the non-Hispanic Caribbean alignment with the West, which is taken for granted by the United States and its European allies, as well as by the "pragmatic conservatism" of Caribbean governments. In practice, the full weight of the U.S. strategic and military presence in the Caribbean appears nearly to be inevitable, abated only by the strategic presence of Britain (which may diminish as talks with Argentina progress on the Malvinas issue) and of France, whose presence is due to its own military role in the European conglomerate.

The predominant security issue during the 1990s will therefore not revolve around containment of a possible Cuban-Soviet threat (though tensions with Cuba may persist), but will focus instead on drug trafficking, seen from the point of view of U.S. interests.

The new drug policy advanced by the Bush administration perceives the region primarily as a fundamental link in the distribution of Latin American drugs bound for the U.S. market and, to a lesser extent, as a marijuana producer and exporter in its own right. The new policy will, first of all, contribute to an increased U.S. presence in the area and to closer ties between U.S. agencies and Caribbean government, police, and military bodies; second, it will lead to a rapprochement with some of the Latin American governments, thus reshaping the region's geopolitical map.

Within this context, the prospects for establishment of a peace zone in the region have been significantly altered. The fundamental elements of a *geostrategic* definition and a *Third World* definition of the Caribbean Basin are also changing substantially and reinforcing existing contradictions between both concepts.

On the one hand, global détente and the reaffirmation of U.S. hegemony in the region are diminishing its geostrategic significance within the framework of East-West confrontation. However, regardless of changes in the international system, certain vital strategic objectives of the United States in the Caribbean Basin—foremost among them the importance of the Panama Canal and the Bush administration's stress on controlling drugs—render unthinkable its withdrawal from or decreased presence in the area. Thus, the view of the Caribbean Basin as an "American lake" is making its reappearance.

Although U.S. economic assistance to the region may substantially decrease in favor of Eastern Europe, the Caribbean is hardly likely to disappear from the list of U.S. security priorities. Improved U.S. relations with the Eastern bloc will, instead, contribute to reinforcing its military options in the Caribbean, with both "low intensity" and conventional warfare backing its interests in the area, as was recently proved in Panama.

Consequently, a great deal depends on the political will of regional actors to contribute to the establishment of a peace zone in the Caribbean or to promote such regional cooperation measures as may be conducive to peace, offsetting the reaffirmation of U.S. military might in the region.

In this regard, both CARICOM and Latin American states appear to favor progressing toward concrete measures to reinforce economic, political, cultural, and security cooperation between both groups of nations. The implementation of mutual trust measures leading to regional disarmament; détente in cases of border conflict, such as in the Esequibo territory; a greater number of bilateral and multilateral economic cooperation agreements, such as the San José Pact; and the political convergence demonstrated in meetings between Caribbean and Latin American leaders all tend to strengthen the process that will lead, eventually, to their taking measures for peace in the Caribbean Basin.[17]

In this context, regional peace and security will once again be directly related to the capacity of regional governments collectively to address the issue of the gap between industrialized and developing countries, attempting to ensure a minimum of socioeconomic, political, and environmental security for their respective societies, whatever the economic difficulties or changes in the global calculus. Despite severe economic problems and radicalization of U.S. hemispheric policy, current political conditions, with democratic regimes prevailing in both Latin America and the Caribbean, should create the appropriate atmosphere for advancing toward a new democratic notion of regional security.

Notes

1. See Sadio Garavini: "The United States, Latin America and Japan: A Virtuous Circle," in *Caribbean Affairs,* 2, 3 (July–September 1989).

2. See Boris Yopo: *América del Sur en los nuevos lineamientos de la política exterior soviética,* Santiago: South American Peace Commission, 1989.

3. Sadio Garavini: Ibidem.

4. *The Daily Journal,* 26 September 1989.

5. Hilbourne Watson: "The Changing Structure of World Capital and Development Options in the Caribbean," paper presented to the meeting of the CLACSO Working Group on International Relations, Caracas, March 1989, p. 36.

6. Humberto García Muñoz: *La estrategia de Estados Unidos y la militarización del Caribe,* Río Piedras, Puerto Rico: Instituto de Estudios del Caribe, Universidad de Puerto Rico, 1988.

7. *El Nacional,* 27 September 1989.

8. See Sutton: "Political Aspects."
9. *Caribbean Insight,* August 1989.
10. *El Nacional,* 12 March 1989.
11. *The Daily Journal,* 7 August 1989.
12. *Caribbean Contact,* May 1989; July 1989.
13. *The Daily Journal,* 20 September 1989.
14. *The Daily Journal,* 20 September 1989; and *Caribbean Insight,* August 1989.
15. The recent meeting organized by the West Indian Committee to discuss the prospects for Caribbean-EEC relations after 1992, held in Barbados in November 1989, fully illustrated the concern of the non-Hispanic Caribbean for this topic.
16. See Jacqueline Braveboy-Wagner: "The Foreign Policy of the English-Speaking Caribbean: Suggestions for Greater Effectiveness," paper presented at the 15th International Congress of the Latin American Studies Association (LASA), Miami, December 1989.
17. The recent meeting of high-level representatives of CARICOM, Colombia, Brazil, and Venezuela in Caracas to discuss cooperation measures in specific fields and the agreements signed by Prime Minister A.N.R. Robinson of Trinidad and Tobago and President Carlos Andrés Pérez of Venezuela in Guiria are clear steps in the direction of increasing cooperation between Latin America and the Caribbean states.

Bibliography

Ambursley, Fitzroy. "Whither Grenada? An Investigation into the March 13th Revolution One Year After." *Contemporary Caribbean: A Sociological Reader,* edited by Susan Craig. Maracas: The College Press, 1982.

Atkins, S. Pope. *América Latina en el sistema politico internacional.* Mexico: Gernica, 1980.

Barry, T., B. Wood, and D. Preusch. *The Other Side of Paradise: Foreign Control in the Caribbean.* New York: Grove Press, 1984.

Barton, John. *The Politics of Peace.* Stanford: Stanford University Press, 1981.

Berkan, Judith et al. "Las violaciones al Tratado de Tlatelolco en Puerto Rico: Un Informe del Colegio de Abogados de Puerto Rico." *Puerto Rico ante la guerra nuclear.* Proyecto Caribeño de Justicia y Paz, Dossier no. 5. (January-February 1985).

Bermudez, Lilia. *Centroamérica y el conflicto de baja intensidad.* Mexico: Siglo XX, 1987.

Boersner, Demetrio. "Una estrategia tercermundista para el Caribe." *Nueva Sociedad,* no. 77 (1978).

———. *Las relaciones internacionales de América Latina.* Caracas: Nueva Sociedad, 1980.

Bond, Robert D. "Venezuela, La Cuenca del Caribe y la crisis en Centroamérica." *Centroamérica. Crisis y Política Internacional.* Mexico: Siglo XXI, 1982.

Boodhoo, Ken I. "Violence and Militarization in the Eastern Caribbean: The Case of Grenada." *Militarization in the Non-Hispanic Caribbean,* edited by Alma Young and Dion E. Phillips. Boulder, Colo.: Lynne Rienner, 1986.

Bosch, Miguel Marín. "The Treaty of Tlatelolco and the NPY." *Nuclear Non-Proliferation and Global Security,* edited by David B. Dewitt. London: Croom Helm, 1987.

Braveboy-Wagner, Jacqueline. *The Caribbean in World Affairs: The Foreign Policies of the English-speaking States.* Boulder, Colo.: Westview Press, 1989.

———. "The Foreign Policy of the English-Speaking Caribbean: Suggestions for Greater Effectiveness," paper presented at 15th International Congress of the Latin American Studies Asso ciation, Miami, December 1989.

Bryan, Anthony. "The CARICOM and Latin American Integration Experiences: Observations on Theoretical Origins and Comparative Performance." *CARICOM Bulletin,* no. 4 (1983).

———. "Commonwealth Caribbean/Latin America Relationships: Emerging Patterns of Cooperation and Conflict." *Contemporary International Relations in the Caribbean,* edited by Basil Ince. UWI, Institute of International Relations, 1979.

———. "Cuba's Impact in the Caribbean." *International Journal* 40 (1985).

———. "The Commonwealth Caribbean/Latin American Relationship: New Wine in

Old Bottles?" *Caribbean Affairs* 1, no. 1 (1988).

Casanovas, Victoria. "Venezuela hacia el Caribe y la Cooperación Sur-Sur" *Venezuela y las relaciones internacionales en la Cuenca del Caribe,* edited by Andres Serbin. Caracas: ILDIS-AVECA, 1987.

Cepal, "Cooperación entre el Caribe y América Latina," E/CEPAL/SES 20/G. 29 (March 1984).

Child, Jack. "Issues for U.S. Policy in the Caribbean Basin in the 1980s: Security." *Western and U.S. Policy Options in the Caribbean Basin,* edited by James R. Greene and Brent Scowcroft. Boston: Delgesschlager, Gunn and Haine, 1984. Quotes are taken from the Spanish edition, Buenos Aires: Grupo Editor Latinoamericano, 1985.

Cintron Tiryakian, Josefina. "The Military and Security Dimensions of U.S. Caribbean Policy." *The Caribbean Challenge: U.S. Policy in a Volatile Region,* edited by Michael Erisman. Boulder, Colo.: Westview, 1984.

Ciricione, J. "The United States Navy in the Caribbean." *Naval Forces* 7, no. 3 (1986).

Clarke, Colin, and Tony Payne, eds. *Politics, Security and Development in Small States.* London: Allen and Unwin, 1987.

Cline, Ray S. *World Power Trends and U.S. Foreign Policy for the 1980s.* Boulder, Colo.: Westview Press, 1980.

Constant, Fred. "Décentralisation et politique aux Antilles Francaises (1981-1987)," paper submitted to the International Colloquium on Eastern Caribbean Geopolitics, Oxford University, January 1988.

Craig, Susan, ed. *Contemporary Caribbean: A Sociological Reader.* Maracas: The College Press, 1982.

Del Alizal, Laura. "Las relaciones de Mexico con el Caribe," paper presented to the CLACSO International Relations Working Group, Puerto Rico, January 1988.

Danns, George. *Domination and Power in Guyana.* New Brunswick, N.J.: Transaction Books, 1982.

———. "The Role of the Military in the National Security of Guyana." *Militarization in the Non-Hispanic Caribbean,* edited by A. Young and D. Phillips.

Demas, William. Introduction to *The Restless Caribbean: Changing Patterns of International Relations,* edited by R. Millet and Marvin Wills. New York: Praeger, 1979.

Dembiz, Andrej. "Definición geográfica de la Cuenca del Caribe." In *Premisas geográficas de la interacción socioeconómica del Caribe.* Departamento de Geografía Economica del Instituto de Geografía de la Academía de Ciencias de Cuba, Havana: Editorial Científico-Técnica, 1979.

Diederich, Bernard. "The End of West Indian Innocence." *Caribbean Review* 13, no. 2 (1984).

Dominguez, Jorge. "Cuba's Relations with Caribbean and Central American Countries." *Cuban Studies/Estudios Cubanos* 13, no. 2 (1983).

Dookhan, Isaac. *A Post Emancipation History of the West Indies.* London: Collins, 1982.

Ely, Roland. "Guyana y Surinam frente al Coloso del Sur." *Venezuela y las relaciones internacionales en la Cuenca del Caribe*, edited by A. Serbin. Caracas: ILDIS-AVECA, 1987.

———. *Olas de las Malvinas: Repercusiones del conflicto Anglo-Argentino en la Cuenca del Caribe.* Merida, Venezuela: Libros Azul, 1983.

Emmanuel, P. "Independence and Viability: Elements of Analysis." *Size, Self-Determination and International Relations: The Caribbean*, edited by V. Lewis. Kingston: ISER, Uwi, 1976.

Erisman, Michael. "Colossus Challenged: U.S. Caribbean Policy in the 1980s." *Colossus Challenged: The Struggle for Caribbean Influence,* edited by Michael

Erisman and John D. Martz. Boulder, Colo.: Westview, 1982.

Espindola, Roberto. "Security Dilemmas." *Politics, Security and Development in Small States*, edited by Colin Clarke and Tony Payne. London: Allen and Unwin, 1987.

Caribbean and Central America. Report to the House of Commons Foreign Affairs Committee. 1983.

Frohmann, Alicia. "Los nuevos parámetros de la política internacional soviética." *Cono Sur* 3 (September-October 1989).

Garavini, Sadio. "The United States, Latin America and Japan: A Virtuous Circle." *Caribbean Affairs* 2 (July-September 1989).

García Muñoz, Humberto. *La estrategia de Estados Unidos y la militarización del Caribe.* Rio Piedras, Puerto Rico: Instituto de Estudios del Caribe, Universidad de Puerto Rico, 1988.

Giacalone, Rita. "Antillas Neerlandesas: En búsqueda de un nuevo Perfil." *Nueva Sociedad,* no. 91 (1987).

Gill, Henry. "Cuba and Mexico: A Special Relationship." *The New Cuban Presence in the Caribbean,* edited by Barry Levine. Boulder, Colo.: Westview Press, 1983.

———. "Granada: La política interna y externa de la revolución. *Gaceta Internacional* 1, no. 2 (1983).

Gill, Henry, and Juan De Castro. "Algunos aspectos de las relaciones comerciales entre el Caribe y América Latina." *Capítulos del SELA*, no. 7 (1984).

Girault, Christian. "Les Caraibes de l'est: Geographie politique d'un archipiel éclaté," paper submitted to the International Colloquium on Eastern Caribbean Geopolitics, Oxford University, January 1988.

Glinkin, A., N. Isakova, and P. Yakolev. *América Latina contra el peligro de guerra.* Moscow: Novosti, 1987.

Goldblat, Josef. *Nuclear Non-Proliferation. A Guide to the Debate.* London, SIPRI, Taylor and Francis, 1985.

Gonzalez, A. "Relaciones Económicas de Estados Unidos con el Caribe." *Capítulos del Sela,* no. 7 (1984).

Gonzalez, Edward. "The Cuban and Soviet Challenge in the Caribbean Basin." *Orbis* (Spring 1985).

Gordon, Marvin F. "The Geopolitics of the Caribbean Basin." *Military Review* (August 1986).

Greene, E. "The Ideological and Idiosyncratic Aspects of U.S.–Caribbean Relations." *Colossus Challenged,* edited by M. Erisman and J. Martz.

Greene, James and Brent Scowcroft, eds. *Western Interests and U.S. Policy Options in the Caribbean Basin.* Boston: Delgeschlager, Gunn and Haim, 1984. Quotes are taken from the Spanish edition, Grupo Editor Latinoamericano, Buenos Aires (1985).

Greenwood, R. and S. Hamber. *Development and Decolonization.* London: MacMillan Caribbean, 1980.

Harden, Sheila, ed. *Small is Dangerous: Microstates in a Macroworld.* London: Davis Davies Memorial Institute of International Studies, Frances Pinter Press, 1985.

Heine, Jorge. "Status aparte: las relaciones internacionales del Caribe 1985-1986." *Las políticas exteriores de América Latina y el Caribe: Continuidad en la crisis,* edited by Heraldo Muñoz. Santiago: Prospel-GEL, 1986.

Heine, Jorge, and Leslie Manigat, eds. *The Caribbean and World Politics: Cross currents and Cleavages.* New York: Holmes and Meyer, 1988.

Hillcoat, G. and C. Quenan. "La iniciativa de la Cuenca del Caribe: Antecedentes y perspectivas." *Venezuela y las relaciones internacionales,* edited by A. Serbin.

Hoetink, Harry. "The Windward Islands of the Netherlands Antilles: Some Recent

Developments," paper submitted to the International Colloquium on Eastern Caribbean Geopolitics, Oxford University, January 1988.

Hurtado, Héctor. "Venezuela and the Caribbean: Integration of Integration." *Studies on the Economic Integration of the Caribbean and Latin America.* Bogota: Association of Caribbean Universities and Research Institutes, 1974.

Ince, Basil, et al. "Decision Making and Foreign Policy: Trinidad and Tobago Decision to Enter the OAS." *Issues in Caribbean International Relations,* edited by B. Ince, et al. Lanham, Maryland: University Press of America, 1983.

International Institute For Strategic Studies. *The Military Balance 1987-1988.* London, 1987.

Jagan, Cheddi. *The Caribbean. Whose Backyard?*

Jaramillo, Isabel. "Problemas de seguridad interamericana," ms., Havana.

———. "Medio Oriente y 'Cuenca de Caribe': Fuerzo de paz o de intervención?" *Cuadernos de Nuestra América* 1, no. 1 (January–July 1984).

Jiri, Valenta and Virginia. "Leninism in Grenada." *Problems of Communism* 33 (July-August 1984).

Jones, Ronald E. "Cuba and the English-speaking Caribbean." *Cuba in the World,* edited by Cole Blasier and Carmelo Mesa-Lago. Pittsburgh: University of Pittsburgh Press, 1979.

Knight, F.W. *The Caribbean: The Genesis of a Fragmented Nationalism.* New York: Oxford University Press, 1978.

Levine, B. "Geopolitical and Cultural Competition in the Caribbean." *The New Cuban Presence in the Caribbean,* edited by B. Levine. Boulder, Colo.: Westview Press, 1983.

Levitt, Kari. "Canada and the Caribbean: An Assessment." *The Caribbean and World Politics,* edited by J. Heine and L. Manigat. New York: Holmes and Meier, 1988.

Lewis, David. "República asociada y/en libertad? El futuro de Puerto Rico." *Nueva Sociedad,* no. 93 (1988).

Lewis, Gary P. "Prospect for a Regional Security System in the Eastern Caribbean." *Millenium* (1986).

Lewis, Vaughn. "Commonwealth Caribbean Relations with Hemispheric Middle Powers." *Dependency under Challenge. The Political Economy of the Commonwealth Caribbean,* edited by Anthony Payne and Paul Sutton. Manchester: Manchester University Press, 1983.

Lopez Coll, A. *La colaboración y la integración económica en el Caribe,* Havana: Editorial de Ciencias Sociales, 1983.

Lowenthal, D. *West Indian Societies.* New York: Oxford University Press, 1972.

MacDonald, Scott B. "The Future of Foreign Aid in the Caribbean after Grenada: Finlandization and Confrontation in the Eastern Tier." *Inter-American Economic Affairs* 38, no. 4 (1985).

Maingot, Anthony. "American Foreign Policy in the Caribbean: Continuities, Changes and Contingencies." *International Journal* 40 (1985).

———. "Cuba and the Commonwealth Caribbean: Playing the Cuban Card." *The New Cuban Presence in the Caribbean,* edited by B. Levine. Boulder, Colo.: Westview Press, 1983.

———. "Las percepciones como realidades: EEUU, Venezuela y Cuba en el Caribe" *Latin American Nations in World Politics,* edited by Heraldo Muñoz and Joseph Tulchin. Boulder, Colo.: Westview Press, 1984.

———. "Problems of a Transition to Democracy in Haiti," paper presented to the Royal Institute of International Affaires, January 1988.

———. "The United States in the Caribbean: Geopolitics and the Bargaining Capacity of Small States," paper presented at the Colloquium on Peace, Development and

Security in the Caribbean Basin. Perspectives to the year 2000, Kingston, March 1987.

Maira, Luis. "Caribbean State Systems and Middle-Status Powers: the Cases of Mexico, Venezuela and Cuba." *The Newer Caribbean: Decolonization, Democracy and Development,* edited by Paget Henry and Carl Stone. Philadelphia: Inter-American Politics Series, Vol. 4, ISHI, 1983.

———. "Los intereses políticos y estratégicos de Estados Unidos en América del Sur," working paper. Santiago: Comisión Sudamericana de Paz, 1989.

Mandle, Jay. "Ideologies of Development." *Transition* 2, no. 1 (1979).

———. *Patterns of Caribbean Development.* New York: Gordon and Breach, 1982.

Manigat, Leslie. "Geopolítica de las relaciones entre Venezuela y el Caribe: Problemática general y problemas." *Geopolítica de las relaciones de Venezuela con el Caribe*, edited by A. Serbin. Caracas: Fondo Editorial Acta Científica, 1983.

Martinez Sotomayor, Carlos. *El nuevo Caribe: La independencia de las colonias británicas.* Santiago: Andrés Bello, 1974.

Martner, Gonzalo. "La Cuenca del Caribe: futuro centro del desarrollo latinoamericano." *Nueva Sociedad*, no. 24 (1976).

Mills, D.O., and V.A. Lewis. *Caribbean/Latin American Relations.* ECLAC/Caribbean Community Secretariat, Oct. 1982.

Mommer, Irama Quiroz de. "La política petrolera venezolana frente a la refinería de Curazao." *Venezuela y las relaciones internacionales,* edited by A. Serbin.

Moron, Guillermo. *Historia de América Latina.* Caracas: Equinoccio, 1978.

Muñoz, Heraldo, ed. *Las politicas exteriores de America Latina y el Caribe: Un balance de esperanzas.* Buenos Aires: Grupo Editor Latinoamericano, 1988.

Muñoz, Heraldo, and Joseph Tulchin, eds. *Latin American Nations in World Politics.* Boulder, Colo.: Westview Press, 1984. Quotes are taken from the Spanish edition, *Entre la autonomía y la subordinación: Política exterior de los países latinoamericanos.* Buenos Aires: Grupo Editor Latinoamericano, 1984.

Parkinson, F. "La crisis centroamericana," paper presented at the Annual Convention of the British International Studies Association, Aberswyth, December 1987.

Pastor, Robert. "Cuba and the Soviet Union: Does Cuba Act Alone?" *The New Cuban Presence in the Caribbean*, edited by B. Levine. Boulder, Colo.: Westview Press, 1983.

———. "The Impact of Grenada on the Caribbean: Ripples from a Revolution." *Latin America and Caribbean Record, 1983-1984*, edited by Jack W. Hopkins. New York: Holmes and Meier, 1985.

Payne, Anthony. "The United States and the Eastern Caribbean Since the Invasion of Grenada," paper presented at the International Colloquium on Eastern Caribbean Geopolitics, Oxford, January 1988.

———. "Whither CARICOM? The Performance and Prospects of Caribbean Integration in the 1980s." *International Journal* 40 (1985).

Payne, A., P. Sutton, and T. Thorndike. *Grenada: Revolution and Invasion.* London: Croom Helm, 1984

Phillips, Dion. "The Increasing Emphasis on Security and Defense in the Eastern Caribbean." *Militarization in the Non-Hispanic Caribbean,* edited by A. Young and D. Phillips.

Portales, Carlos. "Zona de Paz: una alternativa a los desafíos estratégicos de América Latina." *Cuadernos Semestrales*, FLACSO, no. 15 (1984).

Quintero Rivera, Angel. "The Socio-Political Background to the Emergence of the Puerto Rican Model as a Strategy of Development." *Contemporary Caribbean,* edited by S. Craig.

Rebour and Trehard. "Signification strategique de léspace Caraibe." *Defense*

Nationale (April 1986 and May 1986).
The Resource Center. *Focus on the Eastern Caribbean. Bananas, Bucks and Boots.* Albuquerque, 1984.
———. *Jamaica. Open for Business.* Albuquerque, 1984.
Rodriguez Beruff, Jorge. *Política militar y dominación: Puerto Rico en el Contexto Latinoamericano.* San Juan: Huracán, 1988.
———. "Puerto Rico and the Militarization of the Caribbean." *Contemporary Marxism*, no. 10 (1985).
Rodriguez Iturbe, José. "El área vital para la seguridad y defensa y la política exterior venezolana." *La Agenda de la Política Exterior de Venezuela.* Caracas: UCV, 1983.
———. *El Caribe: Elementos para una reflexión política a fines de los 80.* Caracas: Centauro, 1987.
Ronfeldt, David. "Rethinking the Monroe Doctrine." *Orbis* (April 1985).
Rothlisberger, Dora. "Relaciones de Colombia con el Caribe insular," paper presented at meeting of CLACSO Working Group on International Relations, Puerto Rico, January 1988.
Rubin, Vera. "La Cuenca del Caribe y el mar de Simón Bolívar." *Primer Congreso del Pensamiento Político Latinoamericano.* Caracas: Bicentenario del Natalicio del Libertador Simón Bolívar, Tomo II, Vol. VI-A, 1984.
Sankatsing, Glenn. *Social Sciences in the English and Dutch-speaking Caribbean: A Critical Assessment.* Caracas: UNESCO, 1988.
Sedoc-Dahlberg, Betty. "Interest Groups and the Military Regime in Suriname." *Militarization in the Non-Hispanic Caribbean,* edited by A. Young and D. Phillips.
Serbin, Andres. "Crisis política e intervención militar en Granada." *El Nacional,* Caracas, 31 October 1983.
———. *Etnicidad, clase y nación en la cultura política del Caribe de habla inglesa.* Caracas: Academia Nacional de la Historia, 1987.
———. *Etnocentrismo y geopolítica: Las relaciones entre América Latina y el Caribe de habla inglesa.* Caracas: Academia Nacional de la Historia, 1990.
———. "Guyana: Socialismo, etnicidad e ideología nacional." *Politeia* 8 (1979).
———. *Nacionalismo, etnicidad y política en la República Cooperativa de Guyana.* Caracas: Bruguera, 1981.
———. "Las relaciones entre América Latina y el Caribe: Obstáculos y dificultades." *A la espera de una nueva etapa. Anuario de políticas exteriores latinoaméricanas,* edited by Heraldo Muñoz. Caracas: Nueva Sociedad/Prospel, 1989.
———. "Procesos etnoculturales y percepciones mutuas en el desarrollo de las relaciones en el Caribe de habla Inglesa y America Latina." *Boletín de estudios Latinoamaricanos y de Caribe* 38 (June 1985).
———. "Relations between the English-speaking Caribbean and Latin America" *Caribbean Affaires* 2, no. 4 (1989).
———. "Socialismo y nacionalismo en la ideología del Caribe de habla inglesa." *Revista Occidental* 1, no. 4 (1982).
———. "Surinam en el marco regional e internacional." *Anuario de las políticas exteriores latinoaméricanas,* edited by H. Muñoz. Santiago: Prospel, 1988.
Serbin, Andres, ed. *Geopolítica de las relaciones de Venezuela con el Caribe.* Caracas: Fondo Editorial Acta Científica, 1983.
———, ed. *Venezuela y las relaciones internacionales en la Cuenca del Caribe.* Caracas: ILDIS/AVECA, 1987.
Serbin, A., and J. Castillo. *Conflictos limítrofes y proceso democrático en Venezuela.* Santiago: ILET, 1985.
Simmons, David. "Militarization in the Caribbean: Concerns for National and

Regional Security," *International Journal* 40 (1985).

Sunshine, C. *The Caribbean. Survival, Struggle and Sovereignty.* Washington, D.C.: EPICA, 1985.

Sutton, Paul. "EEC Development Assistance in the Eastern Caribbean," paper submitted to the International Colloquium on Eastern Caribbean Geopolitics, Oxford University, January 1988.

———. "Political Aspects." *Politics, Security and Development,* edited by C. Clarke and T. Payne.

———. "The Sugar Protocol of the Lomé Conventions and the Caribbean." *Dual Legacies in the Contemporary Caribbean: Continuing Aspects of British and French Dominion,* edited by P. Sutton. London: Frank Cass, 1986.

Thomas, Clive. "From Colony to State Capitalism (Alternative Paths of Development in the Caribbean)." *Transition,* no. 5 (1982).

Thorndike, Tony. *Grenada, Politics, Economics and Safety.* London: Frances Pinter, 1985.

———. "The Militarization of the Commonwealth Caribbean." Paper presented at the Annual Convention of the British International Studies Association, Aberystwyth, December 1987.

Torres, Héctor. "El Caribe anglófono en el SELA," ms., Caracas: Universidad Central de Venezuela, PhD course in political science, 1988.

United Kingdom. Commonwealth Secretariat. *Vulnerability: Small States in the Global Society.* London: HMSO, 1985.

USIS. *La iniciativa de la Cuenca del Caribe.* Washington, D.C., 1985.

Valenta, Jiri, and Virginia Valenta. "Leninism in Grenada." *Problems of Communism 33* (July–August 1984).

Watson, Hilbourne. "The Changing Structure of World Capital and Development Options in the Caribbean." Paper presented to the meeting of the CLACSO Working Group on International Relations in Caracas, March 1989.

Williams, Eric. "The Foreign Relations of Trinidad and Tobago," address by the Honourable Dr. Eric Williams on 6 December 1963.

Woodward, R. *Veil.* London: Simon and Schuster, 1987.

Yopo, Boris. "América del Sur en los nuevos lineamientos de la política exterior soviética," working paper. South American Peace Commission. Santiago: 1989.

Young, Alma. "The Central American Crisis and its Impact on Belize." *Militarization in the Non-Hispanic Caribbean,* edited by A. Young and D. Phillips.

Young, Alma, and Dion E. Phillips, eds. *Militarization in the Non-Hispanic Caribbean.* Boulder, Colo.: Lynne Rienner, 1986.

Index

About the Book and the Author

Caribbean Geopolitics is a detailed study of exogenous and endogenous factors that have come together to shape the regional geopolitical dynamics after the rise, as of 1962, of non-Hispanic actors in the form of newly independent Caribbean states. Special attention is devoted to attempts at cooperation and integration and to the arms race and militarization characteristic of the region, with particular emphasis on the difficult relations existing between Latin America and the English-speaking Caribbean states. The possibilities for establishing a peace zone are studied in depth within this context and in the light of recent political developments affecting the Caribbean region, a region that has historically been subjected to the hegemonic aspirations and strategic machinations of various extraregional actors.

Through this work, Andres Serbin is providing us with the necessary instruments to identify the specific factors on which action should be based if the desire for peace and self-determination are to become reality in the Caribbean and, indeed, in all of Latin America.

Andres Serbin received his first degree, in social anthropology, at Universidad de la Plata in Argentina. Later, in Venezuela, he obtained an MSC in social psychology at Universidad Simon Bolivar and a PhD in Political Science at Universidad Central de Venezuela.

He is currently professor at the School of Sociology in Universidad Central de Venezuela (UCV). He also holds teaching positions in the PhD course in social sciences and in the School of International Studies at UCV, and is a professor of the PhD course in political science at Universidad Simon Bolivar.

Dr. Serbin was a visiting fellow at the Centre for Caribbean Studies at Warwick University (England) and is a past president of both the Venezuelan Association for Caribbean Studies and the Caribbean Studies Association. He is at present director of the Venezuelan Institute for Social and Political Studies (INVESP) and has written numerous publications on the Caribbean, of which "Ethnicity, Social Class and Nation in the Political Culture of the English-speaking Caribbean " is soon to be available in English.